D0597668

I Wish You Love

CONVERSATIONS WITH MARLENE DIETRICH

I Wish You Love

CONVERSATIONS WITH MARLENE DIETRICH

Eryk Hanut

Translated from the French by
Anne-Pauline de Castries

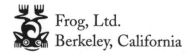 Frog, Ltd.
Berkeley, California

HOUSTON PUBLIC LIBRARY

R0103082616

FARCA

I Wish You Love
CONVERSATIONS WITH MARLENE DIETRICH

Copyright © 1996 Eryk Hanut. All rights reserved. No portion of this book, except for brief review, may be reproduced, stored in a retrieval system, or transmitted in any form or by any means—electronic, mechanical, photocopying, recording, or otherwise—without written permission of the publisher. For information contact Frog, Ltd. c/o North Atlantic Books.

Published by Frog, Ltd.
Frog, Ltd. books are distributed by
North Atlantic Books
P.O. Box 12327
Berkeley, CA 94712

Cover photograph © Turnbridge, 1937, courtesy of the Kobal Collection, New York. Photographs on pages 40, 45, © 1980 M.H.G Archives; all rights reserved © Milton H. Greene Archives. A complete list of photo credits appears on pages 137–138.
Cover and book design by Paula Morrison
Printed in the United States of America
Distributed to the book trade by Publishers Group West

Library of Congress Cataloging-in-Publication Data
Hanut, Eryk, 1967–
    I wish you love : conversations with Marlene Dietrich / Eryk Hanut
: translated from the French by Anne-Pauline de Castries.
        p.   cm.
    ISBN 1-883319-47-1 (clothbound)
    1. Dietrich, Marlene.   2. Entertainers—Germany—Biography.
3. Hanut, Eryk, 1967–   .   I. Title.
PN2658.D5H36   1996
791.43'028'092—dc20
[B]   95-48223
                                                                      CIP

1   2   3   4   5   6   7   8   9 / 00   99   98   97   96   96

For my husband Andrew Harvey

Acknowledgments

MY DEEPEST THANKS to Cynthia A. Cannell, my agent. No words, no matter how carefully chosen, could adequately express my deep gratitude for her presence, help, and support.

I want to thank Marianne Dresser, wonderful editor, friend, and *dame de coeur;* and Lynn Nesbit, for believing. I am also grateful to Anne-Pauline de Castries, my translator; my dear friend Steven Barclay, for endless advice; Gabriel Rabut; Éditions du Cherche-Midi; Éditions Gallimard; Éditions Grasset; Éditions du Seuil; M. Édouard Dermitt; M. Pierre Berge; Simon Chaput; Cindy Spiegel, for helping me understand that my book wasn't complete a year ago; Martha Calhoun; Anton Bruehl, Jr.; Joshua and Anthony Greene; Francine Watkins; Bob Cozensa and the Kobal Collection, New York; Janiece Madhu and the George Eastman House, Rochester, New York; Grove Press; Kathleen Blumenfeld; the staff of *Paris Match;* and the Performing Arts Library of San Francisco.

My deep gratitude and love to Leila and Henry Luce III, for their generosity, love, hospitality, and encouragement; and to Sandra and Douglas Smith, for always loving and caring.

Thanks also to: Anne Teich; Donna Fraser; Kristina Grace; Monique Bezencon; Lauren Artress; Dorothy Walters; Catherine Bensaid; Gilonne d'Origny; Harriet Fields; Sara Foster; Mollie Corcoran; John and Lisa Hunt; Mary Ford-Grabowsky; Gaye Hall; Sharon and Rob Snyder—all of whom made things easier in ways they may not suspect.

Special thanks to Rose Solari, for all her help and love.

To Karen Kelledjian, the faithful heart.

To Kristina Grace, for her friendship, loving support, and help.

To Paula Morrison, for her enthusiasm and talent.

To Caroline and Françoise Bouteraon, with endless love and gratitude.

The dedication page of this book bears the name of my beloved husband, whose love and spirit enrich my life in many more ways than he can ever know. Thanks to my Baby Andy.

And thanks, of course, to Miss Marlene Dietrich.

Marlene, thank you for everything. We did have fun.

God bless you, wherever you are.

Contents

Introduction . . . ix

I Wish You Love . . . 1
CONVERSATIONS WITH MARLENE DIETRICH

Songs of Marlene Dietrich . . . 135

Notes . . . 136

Photo Credits . . . 137

Dietrich: In German, the key that opens all doors.

> *Love's always been my game,*
> *Play it how I may,*
> *I was made that way,*
> *I can't help it.*
> —"Falling in Love Again" (F. Hollander, 1929)

"The real stars of the world are tired of appearing here."
—Marcel Proust

Introduction

"WHEN I'M DEAD, they'll all have known me, you'll see! They'll all have slept with me! They'll be able to say what the hell they want! I won't be there to drag them into court! You wait—it'll be a real bull-fight! I'll be dead; I won't give a damn.... And even you, perhaps, will write *your* book." She added menacingly, "I have faith in you."

Unlike a number of other books about Marlene Dietrich, *I Wish You Love* was not rushed into print at her death in 1992. Dietrich banished from her life anyone who broke the rule of silence she imposed on those she spoke to. Some have avenged themselves by heaping onto her still-warm corpse "whatever the hell they want," just as she predicted they would.

I do not want to claim to be something I am not. I am not a film historian; I am not a biographer. Dietrich hated talking about herself. She dedicated herself to obscuring anything that would not fit with the legend. Don't we all do the same in our different ways?

Who was Dietrich? Who really knew her? No one. She made of her life what the Paramount studio photographers made of her photos—she retouched it. She wanted to bequeath to posterity an Ideal Image. All of those who spoke with her in the last years received a facet of this ideal.

Marlene claimed, for instance, that the sexual power she incarnated throughout her life was "unconscious and invented." She admonished me, "You young people of the Eighties, you see sex everywhere!" What was her truth? What was the truth for one who needed neither to claim nor deny anything, since she was, in some sense, beyond sex?

Who, then, was she? The more I think about it, the less definitively I can answer. I would like to say she was both generous and difficult in what she deigned to give me of herself, that she was a character out of F. Scott Fitzgerald and Dostoevsky at the same time, a creation at once of Feydeau and of Greek tragedy. By dominating fate so imperiously, Dietrich became fate's prisoner. Her face, her voice, bound her fast. She was condemned to deceive so as never to disappoint.

Anyone who is looking for juicy anecdotes should put this book down now. I didn't record our conversations; I took notes, for my own joy. Only once did I neglect to switch off the answering machine after I picked up the phone, and watched it turn around and around. Then I felt ashamed of cornering Marlene like that, and stopped it. A minute or so of her voice, almost intact, remains to me.

I do not really want to write about Dietrich, the Actress. Others have already done so; anyway, we hardly ever spoke about Hollywood. I would like to succeed in bringing to life in this book the woman who, for a long time, gave me advice on what poetry to read and told me of the latest remedies I should take for my liver. And who—without ever being conscious of it—passed on to me a rich cultural and emotional legacy.

"I have faith in you," she said. What could she have meant? It is a terrible responsibility, talking about a dead friend. A responsibility to make her into neither a saint nor a whore, to never lie or mask the truth in any way.

I am happy I wrote this book, because it gave me the chance, for more than a year, to speak again with Marlene. And that, for me, has been priceless.

Eryk Hanut
January, 1996

I Wish You Love

CONVERSATIONS WITH MARLENE DIETRICH

Photo © John Engstead

The lady had passed through to the other side of the looking glass....
Covered in pink and silver sequins, her dress sparkled like a fish that has
jumped out of the water.

THE LIGHTS HAD GROWN DIM. The orchestra, at the back of the stage, had struck up the overture. A medley of unfamiliar airs. I remember a pink curtain—beaded, I think. It was drawn back on either side of the stage, like two open arms, to allow her to enter.

I was eight years old. I was living with a highly eccentric aunt who used to take me to shows children usually do not go to.

The lady had passed through to the other side of the looking glass. She bowed slightly from the waist. Covered in pink and silver sequins, her dress sparkled like a fish that has jumped out of the water. A mermaid's dress. Or a lion tamer's.

She straightened up on reaching the microphone and threw behind her the long train of her swan-feather wrap. Her hair caught the light, gleaming like a pale yellow candle. She was ageless. She *was* time.

She eyed the audience with the semblance of a smile, an expression almost of scorn on her face. Ignoring the cheers of the audience, she raised her hand into the air, pointing a caressing, accusing finger. And then her voice gushed forth, as though from a spring one believed had dried up. Husky, without harshness. Elegantly sensual. Deeply moving, though making no appeal to compassion.

Sunk in a seat that was too large for me, I was petrified by this apparition: part fairytale princess and part retired governess. As song followed song, she would seek a culprit or an accomplice from among the audience, designating him by a glance or by the jut of her chin. She terrified me. I shrank back every time her eye raked the audience. Thank God, she did not see me, and my fear left me when she walked off the stage, only to be recalled to it again and again by a crowd of people who clung to her as to a raft, massing in front of the first row of seats like waves breaking over a rock.

As it was the opening night performance, a big cocktail party was being hosted in the restaurant next door to the theater. The most beautiful women in Paris were there. I had never seen such creatures, with their long, scarlet fingernails, tan skin, and shimmering dresses. They moved with the whisper of crushed silk and the metallic clank of jewelry. I remember a diamond arrow on one woman's breast.

No one knew if she would appear, I was told later. Suddenly, she walked through the crowd of goddesses without seeing them, turning them into penniless fortunetellers by her mere presence.

She floated from one group to another, always with that expression of arrogance, sometimes tinged with tenderness. She would tilt her head back, as though in slow motion, and smile to the other women, who would return the smile, hating her.

She drew closer to where I stood with my aunt. I very nearly bolted. She exchanged a few words with my aunt, who was obviously delighted at her good fortune. The lady glanced at me out of the corner of her eye. While continuing to talk, she chucked me on the chin almost absentmindedly, not roughly but without tenderness. Her light blue eyes, enlarged by the theatrical makeup she still wore, went right through me like a sword. She then turned on her heels and melted into the sea of devotees come to touch the icon.

The following autumn, Dietrich broke her thighbone walking onto some other stage, somewhere in Australia. That was to be her last public appearance. She disappeared forever from the eyes of the world.

Fifteen years later, when I had already been talking to her for months on the telephone, I told her what I remembered of that evening. She did not believe me, protesting that I had been too young. I insisted. She rang off, exasperated.

When I heard this phrase of Dante Alighieri: "There is no greater grief than to remember periods of happiness while living in sorrow," I understood that I had been wrong to insist.

HAMBURG, 1987. I will be twenty in a few days. My gala Parisian evenings are far behind me. I will be twenty in a few days but no one knows. It is of no significance. For far too long, I have been traveling all over Europe. I have not left home; I never had a home. I have lived a lot for someone my age. Too much. And, in fact, I have no age: I have looked twenty-five since I was fourteen.

I take pleasure in what is not even pleasurable, in vacant lots just as vacant as my spirit. Cheap wine, at five Deutschmarks the two-liter plastic bottle, helps me forget the bitter taste of the powders and pills I swallow. All those things that at first make you laugh so much, and then prevent you from crying, or sometimes even make you forget *why* you cry.

I have never asked anything of anyone. I have sometimes wanted to, but I have been afraid of being told "No." I have tried to give something of myself—I have really tried—but I do not seem to know how to give. I live, feeling filthy both in my body and in my heart. I talk to no one. I sleep anywhere. Alone, when I wake up, I drink straight from the bottle stolen the previous day, before the harsh Baltic light blinds me.

I have picked up a tire on the quay, a large rubber tire from a truck, too heavy to float. I make it roll along like a hoop.

This morning, I shaved. I bought myself some new shoelaces for my old tennis shoes. I gaze at the water, at the patches of floating oil reflecting images from the shore.

I have filled the tire with large pebbles. It is really very heavy. I have tied a rope to it. I look at the water. A smell of fish and fuel rises up from the waves breaking against the quay. I tie the other end of the rope round my waist with a very solid triple knot.

A man passes behind me without seeing me. I am as grey as the Hamburg sky. He carries a radio on his shoulder. A woman's voice comes out of the radio. I recognize the voice of that blonde woman I saw one evening, in a theater in Paris, so long ago....

She is singing that she is all alone in a great city—*"Allein in einer grossen stadt...."* The voice disappears into the haze, but the words envelop me. They keep me warm. As though she had just spoken to me. *To me.* To me, who no one speaks to. I hear the echo of my shipwreck in that song.

I untie the rope. I move away from the quay. The water smells too nasty. A shared sadness is better than nothing.

Once more, I have been granted a reprieve.

A month later I am back in Paris. Soon I shall be having regular conversations with the woman who sang about her solitude. And mine.

I never tell her this story. She very quickly teaches me that "it is not done" to talk about oneself.

AT THE END of one of our first conversations, Marlene Dietrich said rather sententiously to me, "Well, I see that you are like me: logical to the point of hardness, and romantic to the point of silliness. Not very promising as far as happiness is concerned!" She then murmured "See you later, little stray," in that intact, astonishingly young voice which set vibrating the cord that links illusion to reality.

A few months earlier, my friend Danielle had taken me to a small movie theater in the Rue des Écoles to see Josef von Sternberg's film *Blonde Venus.* It was a very cold day, and I felt depressed at the thought that it was only the beginning of winter. To tell the truth, I found everything depressing. For years, I had been spending my time wandering endlessly from place to place, occasionally staying with my aunt in her luxurious, soulless apartment close to Bagatelle Park. I slept there, flanked by a Renoir and a Picabia on the walls, a bottle of Johnny Walker on the bedside table.

During moments of lucidity, I read Rilke. His "We are Solitude" resonated within me like the heartbeat of a dying man. I was dying slowly but surely, measuring out my doses of poison with care so as to remain conscious to the end.

Danielle saw me too seldom to be able to realize how close I was to the breaking point, but she was sensitive enough to guess that something inside me had given way. Once or twice a month we would go out together. We had certain tastes in common and this led to our seeing films that were at least fifty years old and plays that nobody else wanted to see.

We were sitting in front of two steaming glasses of hot wine one day, after an outing to see one of Marlene Dietrich's films. I said to Danielle, "That woman is wonderful. I heard her sing on stage when I was little. Is she dead now?"

Danielle knit her brows, frowning out of her beautiful black eyes. "She would be pleased to hear you. She lives here in Paris, opposite the Plaza-Athénée. She is lonely and ill, they say. Why don't you write to her?"

Contradictory as usual, I grumbled, "And why should I write to her?" Then I went home and immediately sent her a letter. A letter which, I was at pains to stress, was not a "fan letter," not ordinary fan mail. As she had spoken to me of her solitude, one evening in Hamburg, I now spoke to her of mine.

With the passage of time, I suspected that my letter was a monument of touching imbecility. She forgave it. But I have sometimes asked myself if her forgiveness was not a refined form of vengeance.

Five days after I had posted the letter, not hoping too much for a reply, the telephone rang. I was alone in my aunt's house, in the big study draped with faded beige velvet. Rain beat against the windowpanes. I stumbled on the carpet as I ran to pick up the phone.

A grave, faraway, husky voice said: "Hallo, this is Marlene . . ."

I immediately concluded that it must be Danielle playing a joke and, not finding it to my taste, I hung up brutally.

A minute later, the telephone rang again. The same voice confirmed, "I really am Marlene Dietrich and you are really very rude."

I stammered out profuse apologies, my heart beating violently. Conscious of the effect she had produced, she reassured me, "People often think it is a practical joke, but I don't always call back."

I will never know why she did call back that day. Today I am totally unable to remember most of our first conversation. She had asked, "What are you doing here, at the moment?"

I stammered that I was just back from Lisbon. I had spent three days there and had arrived back in Paris that very morning.

"Speak a little louder, and stop swallowing half your sentences. I don't know Lisbon."

I told her about the women in their black dresses, the fresh red carnations, the blue mosaics on the white facades. I talked about the Café Brasileira, where Fernando Pessoa used to go. And all those chairs I had brushed against in the hope that I might touch the one he used to sit on.

"Ja, ja, ja. . . . You seem to me to be a real case! How long does the flight take to Lisbon?"

"Er, I don't know ... I went by train, hitchhiking."

"Hitchhiking?! A gentleman never travels by hitchhiking!"

"But, Madame, I am not a gentleman."

"Well, if that's the case, at least try and make others believe you are one! Goodbye."

She hung up. I was to discover that she always did so very suddenly, and I was grateful to her for this, for I loathe interminable goodbyes.

A few weeks later she admitted that she had called again because our first conversation had been "perfectly normal."

"Normal?"

"Well, yes. You didn't aggress me with *The Shanghai Express* and all that old stuff."

For Marlene, asking questions was as natural as breathing. She longed to know who she was talking to, both from curiosity and self-protection. She was at once insatiable and discrete, inquisitorial without being voyeuristic. The brisk Prussian advice she gave would have plunged all the therapists in California into a collective coma. One day, I found myself telling her that I had never before confided in anyone so openly. She murmured slightly—pleased with herself, no doubt—and said, "Before you can kill your demons, you must allow them to appear."

I WAS BORN IN COPENHAGEN, but my family left Denmark when I was not yet two years old. My father was a jeweler, and traveled constantly across Europe, opening up new shops. He must have had many things to forget to keep on numbing himself, as he did, with work, alcohol, and sex. A brilliant talker, my clever father had a fierce penchant for strong drink and easy women. He was very handsome in the peeled, blanched way of a Nazi master swimmer. He married my mother in the Fifties. She was as dark as he was blond. I always thought my parents were very striking, and I still find their looks exceptional. They were like two figures on the prow of a ship.

From the ages of two to five, I lived in Berlin at number 5 Schillerstrasse, and went to the school that was just opposite the house— tall buildings with narrow, dark facades like the ones I was to see years later in Ghent. As I only had to cross the road, no one accompanied me to school. All the other children were taken by their parents. Because their parents were so much less beautiful than mine, I imagined mine to be above all human contingencies of obligation, respect, or duty.

Everything I suffered seemed normal to me. I belonged very early to the statistics of battered children. I never talked about it. I was certain that all this was part of an obligatory ordeal, and that all other children were also beaten. One day when the beatings were a little bit more violent and perverse, the schoolmistress asked me why I was limping. Not at all in a spirit of denunciation, I told her the truth. That evening, my father came to pick me up himself—which had never happened before—and when we got home he threw me again and again against the wall of the cellar until I lost consciousness.

No one believed that people of such high social standing as my parents could also be monsters. Those who knew kept quiet, because my father was powerful in society and could make or break careers. The monster, obviously, was me.

When I was six, we moved one last time to Brussels. There I discovered that God existed. An old servant whose name I have forgotten had great devotion for Saint Anthony of Padua. She revealed to me that God was omnipotent, and that you could ask him whatever you thought you needed most. Every evening I asked, with diabolic candor, for my parents to die. I also remember asking for a white mouse.

I never received a white mouse, but my parents were killed on a Belgian road in July 1974. My father drove his flashy car under the wheels of a truck that was going too slowly. For years, a profound guilt haunted me—I was their murderer. While the lawyers went on and on about inheritances, I was sent to an orphanage. It was officially named the "Home of Welcome," but it amounted to the same thing.

My parents' death stunned me into muteness. I became almost autistic. I did not want to communicate with an external world that had savaged and disappointed me so deeply. It took me nearly a year to begin to speak again, little by little.

One morning, I was ushered into the director's office. The windows behind her were divided into tiny sparkling green and violet squares. She wore her hair in a high tight chignon, and I liked her because she smelled good. She told me, "Your Aunt M. is going to look after you and be your new mother. She lives in Paris. You are lucky, Paris is very beautiful." I had seen Aunt M. two or three times in my life. She scared me a little because she lived far away and always talked too loud. And she was old, too old to be a new mother.

I went to live in Aunt M.'s huge apartment in Neuilly-sur-Seine, a plush suburb of Paris where old actresses go to die. I lived in that apartment for years without ever getting used to it. The red carpets that the Pasha of Marrakech had given my aunt were threadbare. The portrait by van Dongen and Kisling reflected to infinity the same image, the face of my aunt at the apogee of her beauty. She had been a well-known film star, and could not bear the idea that she had survived the death of her fame.

Everything in the decor she surrounded herself with revealed the nearness of death—the large Scottish blankets draping the richly upholstered sofas; the red and gold leatherbound editions of Victor Hugo and Baudelaire, their pages never cut, never read, which I could never touch, and which grew slowly more discolored each summer; the shutters always kept half-closed to protect the Aubusson panels from a sun that hardly ever shone. "They came from the Chateau of Chantilly," my aunt would often say. She also ended up believing that her collection of ancient bottles once belonged to the Empress Eugénie.

When I first arrived at the age of eight, I was astounded by this museum of crystal and velvet. But the years gradually revealed to me the flaking gilt frames, the stained mirrors, the curtains eaten by insects. I hardly ever went to school. The few times I did, the chauffeur would come to look for me because my aunt had decided at the last minute that she did not want to go to Deauville alone.

I had been adopted and taken in to be absolutely and always at her service, a crutch for an old woman to lean on. Terrified by solitude, as I was too, she had given me—without my permission, of course—a role I always found hard to play: that of simply being there. I did not have to be sober or brilliant; I just had to be there.

Until I was eighteen, I was confined to what had been a maid's room, near the kitchen. My aunt used to say to me, "You're so clumsy, I can't rest in peace knowing you are in the apartment. Anyway, the maid's room is perfectly adequate. I myself, during the war,..." and from there, she would sail on to reinvent a role in the Résistance, or wild adventures in the Maquis, or escapes hidden in coal trucks....

Later, my aunt allowed me to take a room in the apartment proper. This was inspired more by her terror of sleeping alone in a large empty apartment than by my age or my needs. My room was very simple: a fabulously heavy Empire bed, a bedside table. On one wall was a painting by Picabia, a grey and ocher portrait of a Spanish woman, half-hidden behind a fan. To the right of my room, there was an office, which became my Ali Baba cave for years—yellowed files stacked everywhere, dozens of pencils and pens plunked together in dirty glasses, and photos lining the faded honey velvet walls. On one wall there was a large etching, a Nativity scene by Dürer. That was the only thing I loved in the whole apartment.

On the immense art deco bureau sat a letter tray, a lamp in yellow and blue crêpe de chine, four beige telephones, only one of which worked, and piles of ancient, empty envelopes, mail from years ago that had never been answered. It was the only place I could be alone; no one else came in there because the radiator didn't work.

For many years, my aunt dragged me with her to her film sets. She relied on me to talk to the technicians, to get the best lighting for her. I understood fame very early, and also understood the relationships between actors, how they rage at each other and make up in the same moment, forced to playact their lives even more intensely when the projectors are off, so as not to disappear.

At fifteen, I knew, far better than I knew geography or history, when the lighting was flattering, when the take was good or not, and could recharge a camera or readjust a microphone whenever necessary. In a pinch, I could in fact replace all the workmen on the set. Very quickly I had learned that when it comes to film images, blinding sunlight is always artificial. I was even stupid enough for a while to want fame for myself, and appeared in a few dreadful films—all forgotten, thank God.

So when Dietrich called me, her voice rising out of the beige telephone like the smoke seeping from the ravine at Delphi, that volcanic vapor dreamed up by the Sibyl, we knew, both of us, from opposite ends of the scale, the dark side of the mirror of fame. We both of us knew, without ever having to express it, that fame is what remains to those who have no luck.

Dietrich could have been everything I most hated, everything I always wanted to get away from, everything I had seen through. But she was far too intelligent to allow herself to be completely cornered by mirrors. By the time I met her, I had lived the extremes of the world she had triumphed in.

My aunt had been a slave to her fame. She had fought hard to grab the best part, and all for nothing. Her only real gift to me was forcing me to grow up in the dust-choked corridors of immense studios—she prepared me, in fact, to begin to understand something of Dietrich.

I often thought my aunt would have been wonderful in the part of Norma Desmond, the forgotten star in the 1950 film *Sunset Boulevard*. But to play Norma Desmond she would have had to step back from herself, and use her own inner chaos to feed and nourish her character. Just like Desmond, my aunt used to order bouquets for herself, and I heard her dozens of times dictating over the phone false messages with false prestigious names attached to them, to be dutifully transcribed onto message cards.

Later, as an adolescent, I myself participated in the sad farce, this *danse macabre*, because she asked me to. I was so invisible, so crushed into the decor, that my aunt could make me a conspirator in her fantasy without any risk of betrayal or even judgment.

My aunt used to say, "Ring my editor, and tell him how you adored my last book! Don't stint on the rapture!" The game was made up of showering her with compliments, like emperors in fairytales who shower their deserving servants with gold coins, and the privilege of participating in it was reserved for a tiny circle of devotees, of old admirers who used a little too much face powder, and young *cinéphile* hairdressers who had had—perhaps only once—the supreme grace of arranging the hair of the ruined Queen.

Once, one Sunday evening, we watched *Sunset Boulevard* together on television. My aunt very quickly left her armchair, in a near hysterical state, and locked herself into her bedroom. For her, the story was "totally implausible" and Swanson was "dreadful." My aunt missed the scene where Max, played by Erich von Stroheim, confesses to Joe Gillis, William Holden's character, that it is he who has written all the fan letters that still arrived at Norma's house.

Forty years earlier, my aunt might have watched the film without any anxiety. To see it again then, as a frail old lady, all too expert at the games of Norma Desmond, and with someone sitting opposite her who had every chance of surviving her, must have frightened her like a red-hot iron.

Sadness chokes me as I write this, sadness for all the failed attempts at love, for my stillborn childhood, for the missed chances, for all the years spent for nothing in a purgatory of feeling that no expiation ever seemed to help me escape.

My aunt never knew I tried to love her. Recognizing that would probably have frozen her with terror, overwhelmed her with responsibilities she never had the inner strength to assume. This shattered woman, who had once had everything a human being can have—wealth, fame, power, prestige, beauty—was not a bad woman, just one haunted by the most terrible of paradoxes: that of wanting at all cost to be loved without ever being able to love anyone.

Did she once have that power? And was it the time she would have had to invest, and perhaps lose, in love that so frightened her?

My aunt continues to live in her vast apartment, alone. We left each other with many bruises, abandoning a past heavy with question marks, but with the one protection that could preserve both of us: silence, and a bastard form of oblivion.

WITH MY JOYLESS CHILDHOOD, I was prepared, when I met Dietrich, to negotiate all the false sides of stardom, and so could steer myself through her legend to arrive more quickly at the real and human person.

Dietrich, like Aunt M., had fought, and fought until the end.

Unlike my aunt, who had been used by fame, Dietrich had used fame like an instrument. And if she had failures, in the end she had been chewed up by no other system but her own. She had understood that the only way to exist in her world was to impose on it her own laws and to refuse to follow any others. She had known the hollow of the wave, but had also always known how to swim out again onto the crest.

Dietrich's career lasted six decades. Once she had reached middle age and had made her fortune, she could have left everything. She endured, however, just as herself.

Marilyn Monroe and James Dean were frozen into icons by a premature death and an unhappy childhood. They never knew the long, universal, active glory of a Dietrich. What would they have become if barbiturates and sports cars as blinding as new knives had not cut them off in full flight?

Marilyn, like Lana Turner or Mamie van Doren, would probably have made cameos in soap operas as a guest star on the fringes of the real. Dean would have been murdered, perhaps, like Sal Mineo or Ramon Novarro, one more pretty young man who faded too fast and whose maturity no one wanted.

Dietrich, then, was not my first star. I lived in an atmosphere of celebrity like a farmer's son lives among cows. In fact, I grew up in a universe, a circus, of more or less forgotten stars. Sometimes my aunt would bring together over dinner old rivals whose wrinkles and triple chins had transformed them into bridge partners. The actors in this theater of shadows formed an impressive cast from before the war.

My childhood was studded with faded stars to whom death would later give back their brilliance. In my first months in Paris, an old woman came to sing Brazilian songs several afternoons in a row. I used to sneak out of the kitchen to listen to her. She had dark skin, and a very obvious wig which slithered down her forehead each time she marked the tempo with the tilt of her head. Her voice, though, was strangely young, rich with sun. But her body seemed exhausted, worn out, and when she leaned against the old Pleyel she melted into it. On the last day she came to the house, my aunt said to me, "Don't forget to say goodbye to Madame Josephine Baker."

A little earlier, in the south of Spain, I met Rita Hayworth. By then, Gilda had short hair and her figure had thickened. She was making a film, her last I think, on the outskirts of the Sierra Madre. She played the owner of a bar, herself a bit lost, who was part consoler of the afflicted, part fortuneteller. She was beautiful, soaked in alcohol and death. Between takes, she used to hug me, take me on her knees and give me marshmallows—the first I ever tasted.

Rita, crushed by the demands of the studios, in the purest tradition of Hollywood melodrama. Rita, whose last directors didn't keep the best takes but only those in which she walked the straightest. Rita, who could only work in the morning because the end of the day found her in pieces, reeling from vertigo in her trailer.

Of those days, twenty years ago, there must remain somewhere a faded snapshot of a sad and lovely red-haired woman in a Seventies-style, short white dress, holding the hand of a young boy, much too small for his age, wearing green pants. Her Alzheimer's was a pretext, I believe; a comforting conclusion at the autopsy. Really, Rita Hayworth died of misery. Like my aunt, she could only survive by drowning in the margins of a reality that only she believed in.

IN A SCENE in *Just a Gigolo,* the last film she consented to make, asking for enough money to live out her days in dignity, Marlene held out a glass to David Bowie, saying: "Drink! It's the best way to forget." No doubt she had her reasons.

I began to drink very early, at twelve or thirteen. Drinking alcohol is a startling thing, like a rain of sand that hardens as it covers you. Alienation by degrees, with a quite definite end. You do not "become" alcoholic; you go from zero to full-blown without realizing how you slid there. One morning, I woke up and understood that the only thing that could make me begin the day at all was a stiff drink. It was as simple as that.

Some evenings, after my aunt's guests had left, I used to slip into the dining room and swallow as quickly as possible the dregs in the glasses left on the table. One day, my aunt came in. Frightened, I let go of the glass, one of her prized pieces of Bohemian crystal, the color of ripe cherry, that always made me want to bite into it when I drank. The glass shattered on the parquet. My aunt screamed, "You stupid little imbecile! You've broken my glass! A museum piece! You are hopeless, hopeless!" The only drama she cared about was the broken glass—not the reason for which I was emptying it so avidly. Nor did she bother to find out why I had recently adopted an odd way of walking, clinging to the walls, or why the bottles in the bar were emptied and disappeared more and more quickly.

She knew that I drank. But she preferred the not-said, the enveloping silence—that great morbid specialty of our crippled family.

My aunt forbade me to sit on her Louis XV easy chairs, but not to have a bottle of Scotch on my night table. She never asked me why I drank. Talking about it would have undermined her domestic system, which she considered beyond fault. (My aunt always believed that her rules were the rules of the world.) Undoubtedly, she was ashamed of my alcoholism, but her shame had no warmth, no concern, in it. It sprang entirely from her passion for keeping up appearances. She never struggled against imperfections; she simply masked them from herself.

From the ages of fourteen to twenty-two, I was heavily under the influence of alcohol. I used to mix Valium capsules that I found in my aunt's bathroom into the dregs of whatever I was drinking. I was perpetually sick, but I had understood that the more I drank the less I would feel any nausea—physical or moral.

I accorded myself certain oases in my hell. Tomorrow was always another day, and always the same. Alcohol offered me rose-tinted glasses. The luxurious hospice and acclimatized coffin I was imprisoned in would start to form constellations of quiet flowers, which, as the hours went by, transformed themselves into enormous mouths, eager to swallow me. Each successive drink calmed them for a while, but it required more and more alcohol to prevent them from biting.

When I met Dietrich, I was prey to chronic stomach aches, nightmares, attacks of boundless emptiness. I tried to stop drinking, without much success. I drank less than before, but I still drank. And I had uncovered in myself a leaning towards drugs of all kinds. I had my personal private mixtures, and knew that the contents of pharmacies and family kitchens can often provide cheap artificial heavens. These linked addictions of mine had made me a corpse, a *clochard* at nineteen. I lived from little temporary jobs, one week working in a garage, the next selling jeans in a flea market, or placing subscriptions by telephone for *Télé Magazine*.

I am not giving away any secret by saying that Marlene drank sometimes, sometimes more than necessary. All her biographers go on and on smugly about her alcoholism. After Marlene's death, many people have told me, with the lugubrious wink of those "in the know," that "Dietrich drank."

I cannot help thinking, "Thank God she did!" Marlene knew that everything was over for her. Her youth had long ago abandoned her, and her legs, which had made her fame, were no longer strong. Can you reproach a cancer patient in the last stages for taking too much morphine? Very few people have lost what Dietrich lost, because very few have had what she had. The people who criticized her are the kind of people who won't give a quarter to a homeless person, on the pretext that they will only spend it on another drink. With one bottle of bad wine, the filthy pavement of a subway becomes a warm bed for a few hours, empty apartments dance with consoling shadows.

Besides, Marlene assumed her destruction totally, without leaning on anyone —just as I did. And who could blame either of us?

She never appeared to me to be drunk, but I used to recognize only too well the way phrases would take time to form, or how a word would hide itself in a mist of champagne. One day, I asked her: "Why do you drink?"

She replied, "You're crazy! I only drink iced tea. I loathe alcohol." And then she put down the telephone and stayed silent for weeks.

She may not have wanted to talk about her alcoholism, but as a kind of revenge, she never stopped asking me questions about mine. She never asked me overtly why I drank, but she loved to find reasons to get me to stop: "Do some sport! That's the way to channel all this dangerous energy," or "Smoke! It's very good to smoke." Marlene was certain that cigarettes didn't do any harm. She had stopped smoking years before, but she adored the fragrance of smoke.

I don't know if the last years of Dietrich were quite as alcohol-soaked as her daughter would like us to believe. I've read her book with care and respect, but the woman I spoke to for hours doesn't seem to be in it. I have never met Madame Riva, but I have great sympathy for her, for I feel that her book about her mother is a cry of never-resolved suffering and I, after all, was not the son of Dietrich. I *was,* however, the nephew of Aunt M., and I know how deep and ineradicable the wounds of childhood can be.

Marlene Dietrich suffered from bearing the mythic name which had long ago stopped corresponding with the old, frail woman she had become. She was a woman who perhaps should never have had a daughter.

∞

PARIS HAS ALWAYS seemed to me to be the epicenter of the solitude of the world. I have always felt in it like a chicken at a gathering of foxes. I am aware that most of my major phobias enter into this rejection. But for me Paris is a kind of poisoned chocolate, a malefic diamond that kills its owners by the glint of its sparkle.

Some people can live happily in Paris, I think. But I never had a foundation on which to build any equilibrium. I knew nothing of myself. Or rather, I didn't know enough to understand, and knew too much to accept.

I didn't know anything about my childhood, about how it was seen from the outside. I continue not to know about many things. I know I had been a blond baby, and who had always been introverted. One of those indistinct children—you don't know whether they are male or female. Perhaps I should have asked the other survivors of my past. But would they have wanted to talk? And would I have wanted to listen?

THE FIRST SCHOOL I went to was in the *quartier* of Passy. I had to cross the Bois de Boulogne by bus. The Bois de Boulogne at seven in the morning is not the most comforting place in the world. Those first weeks I was terrified. Terrified because I was jostled and shoved by everyone, terrified because the driver did not reply to my "Good morning," terrified to miss the stop.

My deep disgust at any kind of school comes from that experience. On my second day I held the two francs I needed to buy a ticket so tight in my hand that the pressure caused them to slip from my grasp and they rolled into a sewer grate.

I went back up to my aunt's apartment and explained to her what had happened. She replied that I was beginning to "ruin" her—strong words have never daunted her—and that if she were to give me two more francs she would only be encouraging bad habits in me. Besides, how could she be sure that I had really lost them? Since I knew the way to school, I could go there on foot. She would write a letter of excuse to explain my being late.

Thank God, I had an ally of sorts: Augustine, my aunt's cook. She looked like Walter Matthau dressed up as a cook. But from the first she had fed me jam crepes, and would sometimes add a small glass of fruit liqueur.

Augustine had found a euphemism to excuse her taste for strong alcohol. Her preferred drinks were all called "lady's liqueurs," and so she could swallow the most revolting combinations with impunity. But I considered Augustine then—and still do—a kind of pagan saint, because she was infinitely patient with Aunt M. Her patience, however, did not prevent her from calling my aunt an "old tart" when she was safe in the citadel of her kitchen. My aunt has always had the extraordinary luck to attract saintly assistants. Working for her more than two months must count strongly among the causes for beatification. She isn't consciously cruel—she has never been—but I am convinced she has never heard about the abolition of slavery.

That morning, Augustine slipped me two franc coins, not without calling down spectacular punishments upon Aunt M.'s head. It was then that I learned the word "whore." I asked Augustine what the expletive "whore" meant and she replied by jutting her chin in the direction of the room my aunt was in. For several weeks, I believed that "whore" meant "actress."

∞

I HAD NO FRIENDS at school. I didn't belong to any group of acquaintances, or any clique. My episodic attendance placed me outside all affective ties, and also cut me off from the ways to create them. I wasn't good enough for the adolescents of Neuilly. To them, I was an orphan who never went to school, who always smelled a little of wine, who never talked to anyone.

Too strange for the people of my *quartier,* and not strange enough for those less socially favored, I became a kind of outcast. That suited me fine, I must say. I always hated talking just for the sake of talking, and so many conversations, after all, come down to just that.

Instead, I read—read constantly, without always understanding what I read. To my aunt, reading was time stolen from life. She considered that aside from reading at night, as a kind of soporific, or in order to learn a role, spending time with a book in your hands was an utter waste, especially when there were always so many things to do *for* her, like spending the afternoon (by royal dispensation) watching *Dynasty* with her and listening to intricate revelations about Joan Collins' make-up.

I used to take down from my aunt's library shelves whatever book came to hand without looking at the title. A bizarre harvest, to say the least, which might yield Colette or Claudel, but also secrets about deep sea fishing or a treatise on locks. I read everything, without skipping a line. I read in the toilet, in my bed, with a little pocket flashlight so as not to arouse Augustine's suspicions (she slept in the room next to mine). She would never have told on me, of course, but apart from finding out about the Windsors, the English royal family, and the princesses of Monaco, Augustine thought reading was useless and just ruined your eyes.

At eleven, I had already read Wilde's *Portrait of Dorian Gray,* Claudel's *The Exchange,* a few novels by Zola. Frequently the sense of the words eluded me, but the music of a phrase would make me drunk with delight, and I would repeat it to myself several times. I talked to myself for hours. I memorized certain expressions I had found in books and I would repeat them all day long, like a mantra, with no connecting thread between these phrases except my passion for beautiful words.

I remember a line of Lamartine that spoke of *repos sublime,* "sublime repose." I used to intone this phrase, followed by *bleu originel,* which I had stolen from Colette. And from some work of Cocteau's, "Those empty glasses that foul up the air." My aunt would pass by and, inclining her head gravely, would say to Augustine that the "drama" of my childhood (when guests were present she would use the expression "frightful tragedy") had shaken me more than one first believed.

Behind the piano (and therefore out of obvious reach) I found a thick volume of Ronsard's *Amours,* illustrated by Rodin, Rops, and Matisse. The fauns and nymphs cavorting in those pages moved me in strange, unknown ways, arousing heat at the level of my solar plexus and lower belly. One day Aunt M. came upon me looking at it, snatched the book out of my hands, shouting, "You disgusting little boy!" and put it back on a higher shelf.

Dismissed to the kitchen, I told Augustine what had happened, and asked her why I had been called "disgusting." She shrugged her shoulders as she did whenever she did not want to give an explanation for something. Then she said maliciously, "Your aunt knows enough about life to read those sorts of books. You don't. Wait 'til later." My always vivid imagination suddenly presented to me the image of my aunt, scantily dressed, being pursued by a leaping creature—half-goat, half-man. Obviously, since Aunt M. knew about life, she must have known about such bucolic pursuits. With her, anything was possible.

To be able to read in peace, I had to be cunning. I offered to clean up my aunt's cellar. It was a completely useless task, but then Aunt M. was obsessed—as I later found Dietrich to be—with the idea of my "doing something." That the "doing" should be beneficial to her in some way, however slight, delighted my aunt. The main thing always was to work for the good of the kingdom.

The cellar was full of empty wine bottles, my aunt's rusty bicycle that hadn't worked since the liberation of Paris, and her old theatrical crinolines that were strewn about, floating and ephemeral like romantic suicides. At least in the cellar I was certain not to be disturbed. Augustine never went down there for fear of catching cold. My aunt never did either because she was afraid of rats. I never saw a single rat.

For years I read everything I could get my hands on down there. Sometimes, I remember, I wept hot, wild tears because a story was sad or simply because it was beautiful. I passed hour after hour there. No one ever thought to check on the work I was supposed to be doing—thank God for the rats—and my aunt's cellar had the unjustified reputation of being the most orderly one in France.

If I were to learn today that the well-to-do apartment building where I spent so many years had just been razed, my only regret would be for that cellar, that dark, dank cellar, its walls streaked all over with the long chalky trails of slugs, and its year-round hollow chill. And for the wild joy that arose from the books I read there, like a warm mist, a comforting smell of clean laundry.

ONE WINTER EVENING, near the beginning of our friendship, Marlene called me very late. "I've just tried to speak to my daughter. The line was occupied. I feel miserable."

Since she had lowered her weapons, I was less reticent than usual. That was perhaps what she was waiting for. "You're asking me heaps of questions," she said. "When I try and ask you, you just fence and shy off. Why?"

I retorted, "Marlene, in your book, you wrote: 'Speaking about myself doesn't interest me.'"

"And you still believe at your age what's written in books?" She was amazed that I had no professional aspirations: "It's not normal!"

"When I was fifteen, I wanted to become a singer."

"My angel, be serious! Can you really imagine yourself singing about hot sand and summer nights and love that fades? Ridiculous!"

"But *you* did it, Marlene."

"First of all, I never sang about hot sand. Secondly, I am a woman. Singing is not worthy of a man, unless you are Placido Domingo. And you aren't!"

I remember that moment—our two voices almost whispering over the telephone in the great empty apartment. She was really listening to me.

"I know your parents are dead.... How did they die?"

"In a car accident."

"How old were you?"

"Seven."

"I also lost my father when I was very small. You can't miss what you've never known. But you were already too old...."

I had opened a locked door, rusted shut for years. At one moment, her voice grew husky, and she called me "my little boy." A mile apart, in a Paris lost in the silence of snow, a young man and the greatest star of all time wept over the wrecked past.

"Don't believe that in killing the memory of your parents you'll make them come back to life. Let them stay dead. It isn't them you have to fight against. It's the child you've never been."

I told her that night about my aunt, my abortive adoption—I had been "welcomed into the home"—no formal adoption had been carried out. And that night, I found myself confessing to her perhaps my deepest fear—that I was nothing. I was no one's son, no one's nephew, no one's lover. My aunt had always driven into me that I was something to be endured, a dead weight.

Marlene sighed gently once or twice, and then said, "Never, *ever* say you are nothing. Never say you are no one. You are my friend, aren't you?"

I caught my breath, and couldn't speak. I was, at last, the friend of someone. That Marlene was who she was meant very little to me; what mattered was the fact that we were friends. What she had just said, I knew, was a vow, a promise sealed forever on that icy night.

She went back to her usual voice. Dietrich had returned. I hadn't known her long, but already, instinctively, I understood her codes. They were my own.

"Now you must sleep. Even if you don't work, you have to sleep." She said goodnight, and then whispered, "Now, even if I die soon, tell yourself you have a long life full of joy before you. Now, wherever you go, something of me will always be with you."

∞

The first photo Marlene sent me.

I NEVER WANTED to be an actor out of love for the alexandrine. I never for a moment imagined myself playing Lorenzaccio or Hamlet. I dream that one day an actor or actress will tell the truth in their memoirs. Enough of this "I did such-and-such a film with director so-and-so," etc. I want a book in which he or she would come clean about their real goals and motives.

I have never met an actor—either famous or unknown—who had a normal childhood (that is, assuming that *anyone* has ever had a normal childhood). People become actors to be loved. I had seen men and women on stage; at the end of the play, people applauded and came to congratulate them noisily. The public *loved* them. It was that simple.

I too had an irrepressible hunger to be loved. I therefore decided to become an actor. People would come at the end of the play and tell me how marvelous I was. My dream.

When I announced to my aunt that I, too, was going to be an actor, she burst out in harsh, mocking laughter. "Everyone will make fun of you," she said. For years that was her credo, her answer to me, whatever my aspirations. She was always in terror of ceasing to be the center of everything, including my dreary existence.

Needless to say, I never had any formal training, never went to a conservatory or official acting school. I had a friend who worked in one of the largest casting agencies in Paris. She got me little jobs in crowd scenes. Because I was tall and thin, I was often used as an extra, wearing a smoking jacket for "elegant evenings." When the pants that I was to wear on the set were too short, the dresser told me not to move too far from the table.

I really believed that I would one day star in a film. I offered myself the luxury of diction lessons with an old member of the Comédie Française. She lived near the Père Lachaise cemetery, in a two-room apartment that smelled of cat piss. She did too, a little.

She made me read the *Fables* of La Fontaine with a pencil in my mouth to get rid of the hint of a northern accent that never completely left me. I think her relationship to the Comédie Française was comparable to my contribution to the cinema. Between failures there often arises a strange kind of collusion. After all, there are no rivalries possible.

Later, my acquaintance Marie-Thérèse helped me get several small publicity contracts for photos in magazines. I was never the "star." I either held an umbrella over a "star model" or opened a hotel door for a "radiant couple."

The triumph of my modeling career was a publicity campaign for Kangaroo underwear. This, too, was one of Marie-Thérèse's miracles. I wore only a pair of white cotton underwear. My body was plastered with makeup. The photographer assured me that my face would not be shown. So far so good. Two months later, I saw myself in a 6- x 15-foot format all over the Paris Metro. That was the only time in my "public career" that people recognized me—my face was all too visible.

I probably could have earned my living a little honestly along these lines. But I waited thousands of hours in "casting" waiting rooms, only to be told most of the time that I was too young, too old, too blond, too thin, too built. . . .

My naiveté during this period was limitless. I had chosen to be an actor in Paris in the Nineties to find some "security." You might as well swim in a pool full of sharks and hope to keep your legs!

My acting work did not exactly fill up my days. I used to walk miles through Paris to dull my pain and boredom, and also to avoid going home too early. My aunt has the particular gift of discerning in someone the quality that can best serve her. A number of friends type her manuscripts, fill out her income tax forms, give her that little quick combing that makes her look like she has just come from the hairdresser. My role was a subtle mixture of all these, with a permanent obligation to be present. For years I obeyed all my aunt's whims. I complied when she asked me, at midnight, to type the last pages of the play she was writing. I crossed Paris to find her the *marrons glacés* she wanted "desperately" and which she did not even taste. I delivered boxes of chocolates to her friends the week before Christmas.

To fill up my time and also for the money, between the ages of seventeen and twenty-three I held every conceivable job—ones that did not require any qualifications, that is. Whenever I had enough money to hold out a month or two, I left and traveled all through France. When I had no more money, I tried to find work wherever I was. And so it went on.

One of my jobs was selling jeans in the street markets. For lack of any written indication, all the jeans were the same size. In the truck, before setting up our booth, we had to sew on the labels which transformed badly-finished trousers mass-produced in Taiwan into "authentic" Levi 501s. When clients expressed their amazement at such low prices, we had to tell them, "Ah, the jeans were seized by customs, the boss has a cousin who's a customs officer." And people would snap the jeans up, flushed with the thrill of buying a bargain and slumming a bit. Since these jeans didn't keep their shape after the first washing, you had to make sure that you never went back to the same place twice.

I was engaged officially as "Under-Gardener of the City of Paris." I really loved that job. I was the only white person on the whole team. I worked for several months in the parks, planting petunias or ornamental sage bushes. There were rules that had to be respected, for instance, not to get mixed up in the work of the park guard. If you swept up dead leaves in his place, you ran the risk of trouble with the union.

I also decked out all my aunt's balconies with geraniums—I had to give her little pleasures to excuse my daily desertion. Actually, she appreciated them and every evening after I had watered the plants, she would exclaim, "How well they grow, you can tell that they come from the Hôtel de Ville!" Since my aunt adores everything honorific—*lègion d'honneur,* war medals of every kind, "keys to the city," etc.—geraniums from the town hall of Paris couldn't be anything but more abundant. Obviously.

I washed dishes in countless second-rate restaurants, an idiot's job, easy and quite well-paid if you don't have many needs. I also sold books—the last copies of unsold editions that no one bought even when they were going cheap. There you had to watch out for the competition of the booksellers on the quays who didn't fool around when it came to legal permits.

What amazes me still is that I never fell into the web of prostitution. The opportunities were there, at times, but I never seized them. It wasn't really a question of "purity" or "honesty." These, for me, have always been relative. Rather, I have always thought that in order to find yourself in bed with someone, something authentic must pass between the two of you. Something that no amount of money or "favors" could provide. And also, not selling my body was perhaps my ultimate way of staying as alive as I could, of never ceasing to belong at least to myself.

∞

IT TOOK ME some time to realize that one of the great legends of the century was telephoning me regularly.

I was not aware of Dietrich's importance. I knew very little about her, and this put our relationship on a much more relaxed footing. If she were to call me up today for the first time, my admiration would probably make sincerity more difficult. My devotion to her grew little by little. She was pure, like the ideal of some pagan cult, innocent of any dogma. And our relationship probably also owed its longevity to our having kept our eyes wide open.

I soon understood that she was emotionally paralyzed, that her soul was severely scarred. She spoke in short paraphrases, scathing like the whistle of a bullet. She only said what was essential. Without emotion. But each word had incredible human density, attesting to a full, rich, and well-lived life.

She generally called me up after lunch, though not actually out of respect for any particular code as far as time was concerned. She sometimes woke me up late at night to tell me I ought to reread

Goethe's *Pandora*, for instance. Her voice was deep, but she modulated it at will and could, on memorable occasions, give it a mellow, almost *powdered* tone, as one says of certain rare scents.

Though many light-years apart, we were two solitary misanthropes who had found in each other a mirror. We talked often of anything and everything, and sometimes of nothing at all. I would tell her about my life; but, above all, she would tell me about her past, repeating anecdotes she perhaps embellished, holding me spellbound as she had, in former times, her audiences, orchestrating her effects with the subtlety of a Siamese cat.

As strange as it might sound, I always knew when it was Marlene ringing. It isn't that I was waiting for her call; I wasn't waiting for anything. But as some people have a recognizable walk or a particular way of knocking, Dietrich's way of telephoning—from the moment the phone rang to the moment she put it down—was like no one else's. It was commanding, imperial. The phone seemed to be saying, "Pick up immediately! It's me!"

She would say, "Hallo," and then leave a space, as if to receive a salvo of applause. Her "Hallo" floated, unraveled like a roll of old Chinese silk, or like heavy taffeta sweeping across waxed parquet. Then she would add, "It's Marlene." Eventually, all she would say was, "It's me. Is that you?" This secret code, this amateur spy dialogue, brought us more closely together than any polite formula. Its tender anonymity was who we were.

"What have you been doing with yourself these last few days, my angel?"

She would put this question to get the conversation going. But our conversations were usually a Dietrichian monologue. She first called me "my angel" one lucky day when she decided that I had the "voice of an angel." She pronounced it in tones soft as cashmere. Conversely, on the rare occasions when she called me by name, she did so in a dry, almost impersonal, manner.

"It's funny, your calling me 'my angel.' I do the same thing with my dearer friends."

Her "Hallo" floated, unraveled like a roll of old Chinese silk, or like heavy taffeta sweeping across waxed parquet.

"Oh, yes? Rilke said: 'Every angel is terrible.'"

"Yes, I remember, it's in the second 'Duino Elegy.' How are you, Marlene?" She had told me—ordered me, in fact—to call her by her Christian name one day when I was jumping from "Madame" to "Mademoiselle" without being able to decide on which one to use.

"I survive. What else can I do? Life is nothing but a long sort of blackout in which to forget life.... Are you in love?"

"No."

"How strange...."

"What?"

"That anyone would be able to live without being in love, as though love did not exist. *Gott,* when one has once had the luck to love, why should one ever have to open one's eyes, come to one's senses?"

I ventured timidly: "Perhaps if one kept them shut, love would disappear?"

"Shut up! You're not in love! You are incomplete! Sometimes, if one opens one's eyes, love also disappears. Only time can tell."

"Don't get annoyed, Marlene. We are two solitary creatures. Why should we quarrel over love?"

"*Ach,* but I am not quarreling with you. I am trying to get you to be yourself. How can you allow yourself to speak to me like that? You are not even born yet!"

"Let's not be melancholy. Not tonight. It's such a beautiful evening. I am leaning over the balcony and I can see the lights of the cars shining through the trees in the Bois...."

"Pooh, literary nostalgia! Under what sign were you born?"

"Gemini."

"Oh dear! In what year?"

"1967."

"*Gott,* is it possible to be born in 1967?! Do you like champagne?"

"Yes. But I am not much of a connoisseur...."

"Ah, but one must be! The best champagne in the world is Le Crèmant Blanc de Blanc. It's the one I like best, too. But there is no point in talking about it, as you are not a connoisseur. Try and remember

Photo © Erwin Blumenfeld

After every conversation, Dietrich would stroll through my mind, grace-fully, like someone taking stock of their surroundings, visiting. A queen in exile.

this champagne, nevertheless.... A phrase keeps running through my mind. Who said: 'Happiness one remembers is no longer happiness, but the memory of pain is always pain'? Do you know who said that, my angel?"

"Er ... that sounds like Byron, doesn't it?"

"Really? Perhaps.... Anyhow, I don't really care. See you later."

I NEVER TRIED TO MEET HER. I did not see the need for it. Marlene lived hidden from sight—a paradoxical seal of secrecy for someone who had so often allowed her image to be stolen. The voice on the telephone was that of the woman in the films, of the face veiled in cigarette smoke. I never imagined her otherwise.

After every conversation, Dietrich would stroll through my mind, gracefully, like someone taking stock of their surroundings, visiting. A queen in exile. I had only that voice, half-seaweed, half-star; the voice of Circe, and that of a rather rough little girl out of some fairytale by Selma Lagerlöf.

From this voice rose the ritual of seduction, free of visual constraints or any need to strike languid poses. A verbal bullfight, in which we each in turn played the bull.

Once, and once only, she suggested to me, in an unusually playful mood, "We should have tea together one day. I want to find out if your manners are good."

In short, the old game of "who loses, wins," at which she was exceptionally skillful.

I tried to sound as casual as possible, though I was quite dumbfounded: "Yes, of course ... perhaps later on...."

The reply she was expecting.

The dream remained intact. She kept her power. We never broached the subject again.

∞

MARLENE WAS INTERESTED in other people. I can say without vanity that she was interested in me. She wasn't glitzily political in the age-old show-biz way, she didn't sign petitions for the latest fashionable "cause," or have herself photographed with the Dalai Lama to pretend she was mystical. But she paid the rents and medical expenses of her poor and sick friends, which is surely more glowing in God's eyes. And she, herself, never scavenged for sympathy. I admired her for that. She despised easy publicity, she mocked the front-page fluctuations of Liz Taylor's weight, and despised Taylor's lack of reticence.

For a long time, Marlene had been insisting that I send her a photograph of myself. I didn't want to do it. I was shy, no doubt, but also I couldn't see the point. Dietrich had already communicated to me an unshakable logic: certain things were simply "not done." I thought that it "wasn't done" to send her my picture. I didn't find myself "photogenic," I told her.

"I don't need your photo to offer you a star role, I want to know what you look like. Don't I have a right to know?"

I finally sent her a photo. She called me up immediately.

"My angel, you have wonderful eyes—but," she paused, "do you really love me?"

"Yes, of course, I really love you."

"Then, put the phone down."

"Why?"

"Put the phone down, and burn the dreadful shirt you are wearing in the photo. I dare not imagine the risks you run wearing something so horrible."

"But I love that shirt!"

"I can forgive you for not having any taste, but not for being crazy. Burn it!"

I didn't burn it. But I threw it out a few weeks later, which amounts to the same thing.

Dietrich then began to give me courses in elegance. She became for me what Proust said Montesquiou was for him — a "professor of beauty." At the time, I didn't recognize the hidden motherly tenderness in what she did. Now, when I think of it, tears come to my eyes.

"I know you have no money," Marlene said once, "but money has nothing to do, you know, with good taste. You should wear white, black, or blue shirts. Nothing else. You can find them in department stores. I'm not asking you to shop at Lanvin!"

It was the first time anyone in my life had talked to me like that. It's true I dressed badly. Actually, I didn't "dress" at all. No one had ever told me that brick-red trousers don't go with a blue shirt.

Today, all of the clothes in my wardrobe are chosen with the taste Marlene taught me. Often, I take down a shirt in a shop, and return it to its rack, saying to myself, "Not that one. She wouldn't like it."

I didn't blindly take her advice, though. One day she decreed that Guerlain's Habit Rouge was the only eau de toilette for men. I said that I hated the smell.

"That's not normal! You *must* love Habit Rouge!" And she immediately sent me a large package with all the Habit Rouge products, the whole lot—cologne, soap, shaving cream, talc, bath oil.

Dear Marlene, the few lies I told you were white lies. I continue to loathe Habit Rouge. As you would say, "It's my right, isn't it?" I gave away the contents of the package, and perhaps the people I gave them to didn't like them either. You left this world thinking I loved that perfume. You even added, "I was *sure* Habit Rouge was for you!"

∞

SHE INUNDATED ME with photographs furiously initialed in black, gold, or silver. I felt, on looking at her signature, that she was still the same changeless but erratic creature she had ever been. A beauty as

Photo © Laszlo Willinger

"Money has nothing to do with good taste. You should wear white [and] black."

no interest to anyone. There's no reason why those people should make money at my expense. I don't want it."

"Marlene, no one's going to make money at your expense. I am lending my photographs. I am not renting them out. And the museum is handing the profits over to charitable organizations."

"No. Don't insist."

Somewhat to my annoyance, I had to inform the museum director of Marlene's decision.

Very early the next morning, Marlene called me: "I've thought it over. If that exhibition is really philanthropic, and since it seems to give you so much pleasure, I agree."

But during the following days, she changed her mind so many times that I finally had to read her the riot act: "Marlene, those people have a job to do, and they are doing it well. It's sheer amateurism to change your mind all the time as you're doing. Say yes or no, but stick to your decision!"

"Me? Amateurism?! No one has ever dared speak to me like that! You little fool!" And she hung up, furious.

I had struck a nerve. Nothing could have insulted Marlene more profoundly than to put her professionalism in doubt.

An hour later, she rang back, her tone very cold, as though she were talking to someone else: "Please send me xerox copies of all the photographs you have of me and I'll make the choice myself. How many do they want?"

"About fifty."

In English, she grumbled, "God, these people are too smart. . . ."

The exhibition was a great success. Marlene had chosen a photograph from *The Shanghai Express* for the poster. A strange coincidence, almost an omen, for it belonged to the same series as the photograph which was to appear nine months later on the poster for the Cannes Film Festival. That image, displayed all over the city, was to be the backdrop for Marlene's last journey from Paris.

The evening of the exhibition preview, Marlene called me at the museum gallery. She wanted to know about everything: the quality of the champagne, what the guests were like, etc. She insisted on speaking to the manager and gave him a three-minute lesson in photography, inquiring about the lighting, the way in which the portraits were framed.... After he hung up, the poor man confided to me, quite overcome: "She is fabulous! Thank God, I've already made my speech. Otherwise, I wouldn't have been able to say a word!"

SHE HAD CHOSEN to burn herself in the light of her own flame. I respected her for it.

"Each bird has the color of its call," wrote Malcolm de Chazal. Dietrich was the color of fire. A fire that still has the power of illuminating our darkness.

Almost everything there is to say about Marlene Dietrich has been said. Except, perhaps, that her aesthetic journey through time has only just begun. And that, as she herself taught me without knowing that Rilke's phrase both condemned and vindicated her: "the Terrible always has its beginning in Beauty."

"AND WHAT IF we were to talk about jealousy?"

"What sort of jealousy?"

"Jealousy in love, of course, not envy...."

"I think jealousy is as necessary to love as love itself."

"But, Marlene, what about trust?"

"Leave trust out of it! Trust has nothing to do with love. It's vigilance that's important."

"Nowadays, jealousy seems a very outdated concept."

"Let's talk about it! All that happened after May '68. One had everything for the asking; everyone slept with everyone else! That

Photo © François Gragnon, Paris Match

Inevitably, Marlene dubbed this photograph "The Death of the Swan."

so-called 'free sex' is more imaginary than real. It's a fashion. To lose interest in the fate of the couple would, in the longer or shorter term, lead to general disaster."

"You mean the couple in a heterosexual sense, from the Christian point of view?"

"A couple is a couple. A normal human being is not capable of living alone."

"Even couples of the same sex?"

"People of your generation always amuse me with their silly notion that they have invented everything! When I was young, in Berlin, homosexual couples were a common thing. Don't try and tell me that your generation has opened every door, O.K.?"

"Nevertheless, tell me what you think, Marlene."

"I don't know, there are people who love each other, and that is that. Those who just make love, that's a neurosis. . . . But, now, with that bloody illness, it's like walking on a tightrope! Real love liberates from the flesh: you are no longer a slave to your senses, for you sleep with someone you love."

"But you do realize, don't you, that a large part of your public is gay?"

"Of course I know that! And so what? They have turned me into an androgynous Madonna, and all those things in magazines. Rubbish! When one is an artist, the only thing that matters is that people should like one's work. They like my work, that's fine. Who they sleep with is none of my business."

"To go back to jealousy. . . ."

"Ah, yes. . . . Well, what I said to you about liberty sums up what I feel. I am convinced that giving to a partner all the liberty that he or she asks for simply means endangering the happiness of both. It's building on sand. Modern couples 're-choose' each other. It's their own business if they want to play with fire and burn themselves, but they mustn't then come and complain afterwards. The woman who authorizes her husband to go out with another woman—or the opposite, for that matter!—has no excuse. A couple belong to each other.

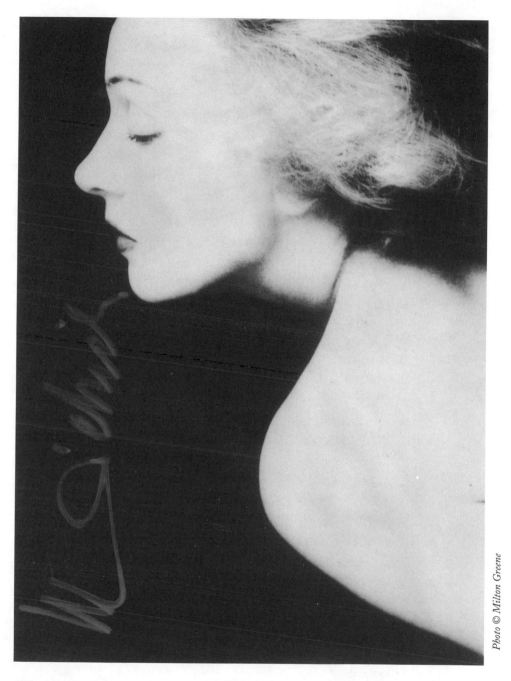

Photo © Milton Greene

"You prefer the ones taken on rainy days. My Zen photographs."

Photo © John Engstead

Almost everything there is to say about Marlene Dietrich has been said. Except, perhaps, that her aesthetic journey through time has only just begun.

All other solutions are grotesque. What stability can you expect in a planet peopled by men and women who betray one another?"

"It is a very interesting point of view...."

"It's not a 'point of view'! It is the truth! People who are unfaithful to their partners don't realize that they are the first to be betrayed. I have the greatest contempt for them. How sordid their pleasure must be. Our salvation lies in fidelity. And now with AIDS, this is more than ever true. All those people who catch this virus, now that everyone knows how it is transmitted, simply get what they deserve."

"Don't be so awful!"

"And you, stop playing at being broadminded, it doesn't suit you in the least! I am not odious. I am not talking of those poor unfortunates who have been dragging themselves about for the last ten years, nor of those who have had blood transfusions.... But I feel no pity for those who have a regular partner, who are unfaithful to them, and then catch the disease the following night."

"You are speaking about death, Marlene, be careful."

"And what about them? Don't they realize that they can kill their partner with their unfaithfulness? Lies have been responsible for the deaths of more people than machine guns! Sleep around with all Paris if you are free, and good luck to you. But if you are bound to someone, have some respect for them at least, even if you've none for yourself."

"Or else?"

"Or else? Get yourself castrated, like the bulls!"

∞

"THERE IS SOLITUDE. Jean Cocteau once said, talking about my solitude, that I had 'chosen it.' He was right."[1] She wrote these lines in 1984. She had been a recluse for eight years, and had eight more years to live. These words seem to me to be full of pathos, of retrospective greatness. How does one have the strength to retire from the light, when one has taken refuge in it for so long?

She was alone—profoundly so. She was adamant in refusing all outside help. "No one can preserve their solitude who does not know how to make themselves odious," wrote Cioran. She managed her life from her bed, and had decided to live through her purgatory unaided. What some took to be ill temper, I felt to be no more than a final and formidable assertion of independence. And with it she proved the truth of her friend Hemingway's phrase: "Courage is grace under pressure." No self-pity. Ever.

One day when I was complaining—a bit too insistently—of a persistent but mild toothache, she changed the conversation. Referring to a bloody though distant war, she declared in a sour voice that compared to that, "our little Western miseries" left her cold.

I shall never forget this lesson.

From early childhood she had received a very strict upbringing. Rimbaud said of his mother that she was "more inflexible than seventy-three leaden-helmeted civil servants." Frau Dietrich's mother also fits this definition. The childhood pages of Dietrich's memoirs are full of precepts that would cause any modern child psychologist to faint. "In our Christian society," she writes, "one learns to hide one's feelings. I have grown into a woman who never reveals her innermost feelings, an aloof and lonely woman, imprisoned in the sanctuary of her 'sufferings.'"[2]

Further on in the book, she stresses that "keeping a tight rein on my emotions had become second nature.... I knew that the first, most elementary, rule of conduct was to bear the inevitable with dignity. The tears one sheds over what is inevitable must always remain secret tears."[3]

Dietrich relates how she received her last maternal slap on the evening of a ball at which she had refused to dance with a young man she disliked. Her mother had taken her aside, slapped her, and told her in no uncertain way that "even if she didn't like him, there was no need for everyone to know it."

Marlene had a habit of declaring in a peremptory tone: "It is not done." During our last conversations, this phrase became almost obsessive. I feared she would one day tell me that talking on the telephone "is not done."

Can we be surprised at such a woman having chosen to seclude herself for life?

If her dear friend Louis Bozon worried about her having apparently caught a cold, she would immediately bark: "Who has said anything about a cold?" and put an immediate end to the discussion.[4] In 1988, she gave an interview to *Figaro*. To the tactless question, "Is it true you no longer go out at all?" she had replied: "Of course not. I go to the country, to stay with friends. There, nobody bothers me. It is true I no longer walk about in Paris, but it would be completely absurd not to go out at all."[5] She stated this with the glacial composure of a Prussian officer's daughter, though she had in fact not left her bed for nearly ten years.

She disapproved of giving any indication of your state of health. In a pinch, you must lie about it. A lot of old people lie so as to be pitied. Dietrich lied so as *not* to be pitied. At the end of her book, speaking of the fractured thighbone which had confined her to her bed for good, she wrote: "I have remained very stiff, but I manage to walk through sheer force of will.... Since then, dozens of men and women have written to me telling me of their 'immense affliction.' It is very sad; I, on the other hand, do not feel particularly afflicted. I walk with a limp, but that is not a disaster, and those who really love me find my gait quite interesting."[6]

She sent me her book and I laughed a lot on first reading it, recognizing Marlene's scathing wit. I later understood how tragic these lines were, because by the time they were published she had been unable to walk for some time. But to mention this was "not done."

"DO YOU KNOW 'The Flag'"?
  "What flag?"

"*Ach!* 'The Flag' by Rilke, of course!"

"I know Rilke wrote a poem entitled 'The Flag,' but I have never read it."

"*Ach!* That's unspeakable! Terrible! You claim to know Rilke…"

"I don't claim to know Rilke, I claim to like him. That's different. And that poem doesn't appear in my edition, that's all."

"All the translations of Rilke are frightful, all of them. Don't you have his complete works?"

"No."

"*Ach!* That's terrible, terrible!"

I was getting ready to answer when I realized she had slammed down the telephone. I did not call back. To hell with her! And to hell with all Rilke's translators.

A little later, the door bell rang. It was a delivery man from one of the larger bookshops on the Champs Élysées.

"But I haven't ordered anything!"

"The bill has been settled, sir. It is a gift."

I extricated three thick volumes from their brown paper wrapping: Rilke's prose, poetry, and correspondence.

Her voice, still saturated with anger, answered me at the other end of the line.

"Thank you, Marlene. But you shouldn't have. Really, I am quite overcome."

"You shouldn't feel overcome, but ashamed not to know all Rilke. From now on, you'll definitely be unforgivable."

And she hung up.

DURING THE LAST YEARS of her life, Marlene severed a number of sentimental ties. All those closest to her were forced to face the killing fields of friendship. Did she want to spare them the vision of a broken idol? Or did she simply feel that she had done her bit?

Robert de Montesquiou once wrote, in reply to an invitation, "I used to love being seen, but I no longer enjoy it. One only likes doing what one does well, and there is a time for showing oneself." Marlene, who detested high camp literature, certainly had not read those lines. Did she make herself invisible so as to defend her private life, or to maintain her legend?

Dietrich's greatest role was an amalgamation of the two. She sang, *"I want to buy some illusions."* She elevated illusion to a form of aristocracy. It was not so much that she lied, but that she had her own sublimated version of the truth.

Reading Kirk Douglas' memoirs, some time before her death, she cried out angrily: "That son of a bitch writes that I am an invalid! That's going to make things difficult for me with the insurance if I am offered a contract."

To what extent did she deceive herself? She told me that Remarque would quote Scriptures to her: "Give me the strength to stand upright, with my head held high, even when I am alone and no one is there to see me." And these words had often been of great help to her, she who lived without God. It seems to be the common lot of those who have enchanted crowds to spend their last hours in solitude.

She had written, in a passage on Hemingway: "When our bodies no longer respond as well as they used to, when our brains no longer work, it is time to take our courage into both hands and blow out the candle."[8]

She let the flame dwindle a long time before it finally died out one afternoon in May. It was constantly necessary to cloud the issue. She imagined she could imitate the voice of her housemaid and would tell unwanted callers that she was at Dior's, at the doctor's, in Japan....

During a radio interview in 1962, she declared: "The end of my life will be no *Sunset Boulevard*. Even if I stop working, I will always find something to do. People who retreat into their memories must be rather second-rate." Thirty years later, her conversation was punctuated with the words "ugly, ugly, ugly." This word summed up all the despair with which she looked on a world she no longer recognized, from which she fled with the anguish of a drowning man, both in terror and with the promise of the depths. She no doubt saw isolation as her last chance, a masterly "final curtain." From it, she continued to build up the Dietrich legend, as Proust—whom she loathed—had written his *Recherche du Temps Perdu* with the frenzy of an invalid who knows his days are numbered.

MARLENE DEVOURED EVERYTHING that appeared in the international press. Absolutely everything. Which meant that she was remarkably well-informed as far as politics, fashion, and the misfortunes of princesses are concerned.

Sometimes in the midst of a discussion on Rilke, she would, with the perverse pleasure of an old lady who has decided to slum it, slip in a few words: "I do think Prince Charles is behaving very badly towards that poor girl. It's true she doesn't look awfully bright, but he did marry her. Ah, all that gossip, it just isn't done."

Marlene, who did all she could to avoid any intrusion of the media into her own life, was perversely titillated by all the indiscreet revelations on the private lives of kings. She was really the most contradictory person in the world. But she very soon lost interest in English royalty, and took inordinate delight in gossip about Monaco. Princess Stéphanie had for some time been her whipping boy.

"That Stéphanie is a menace—she is making a record! Why doesn't she do her job as a princess and inaugurate hospitals? Why does she insist on singing?"

I would reply that the money collected from the sale of the records went to charity.

She would fire back: "Poor things! The Salvation Army and cancer research really don't deserve such a fate."

For a long time, Stéphanie de Monaco's evil reign held sway over

Marlene Dietrich's days. If the previous evening's fashion show had displeased her, she would exclaim: "Naturally! That awful Stéphanie dresses like a housemaid who has won the lottery, and everybody copies her! What an epoch!"

If the variety program had bored her, it was: "Since that silly goose from Monaco has taken to singing, it's become the fashion to have as little voice as possible. Madonna at least is above that!"

For now Marlene had decided to admire Madonna, as inexplicably as she hated Stéphanie de Monaco. "She sings badly and is very vulgar, but her show is impeccable. The public never makes a mistake."

Having learned that a nightclub near Avenue Montaigne was patronized by Princess Stéphanie, she took to blaming her for every street noise, every honk of a car horn, that reached her ears: "Since that awful Stéphanie has taken to dancing near here, life has become impossible."

I did not try to dissuade her—it would have been quite impossible. And, quite frankly, I found her phobia amusing. The morning of the Gulf War ultimatum, in January 1991, I thought that once the shock had passed Marlene would surely call me up and blame the conflict on Stéphanie de Monaco. She did not. But she was quite capable of having thought it.

December 28, 1990. Marlene rang me up very early: "Honey, I am not wishing you a happy Christmas, because I simply hate it. And I must say I don't know anyone who does enjoy it. All those rowdy binges 'round an event which is supposed to be divine! What an epoch! But I wanted to tell you that you have all my best wishes for next year. And thank you for your sweet card."

The day before, she had celebrated her eighty-ninth birthday. The whole world had talked about it. Which she hated. I had sent her a simple, brief message: "I, too, am thinking about you." Just so she would know.

A week earlier, she had declared: "If you really love me, don't send me any flowers. Buy yourself a good book and think of me while reading it."

"Why?"

"Everyone sends me flowers on the twenty-seventh of December! I loathe cut flowers. At this time of year, I can't open the windows of my room and the scent goes to my head. Think about me—I'd much prefer that."

"You don't like any cut flowers?"

"Yes, tuberoses. But they never look as beautiful as they do in a Provençal garden, at the close of day.... However, I will never again see them like that...."

Someone else would have added "alas," or "what a pity." But not Dietrich. Her statements were purely factual, without superfluous commentary.

I obeyed, and that morning she thanked me: "My apartment looks like a chapel. It gives me the feeling of being already dead. And flowers are so expensive at the moment—those people must be mad!"

"Those people love you, Marlene."

"Pooh! Out of twenty bouquets, five have been sent to me out of affection; the others come from people who simply want to be able to boast that they've sent me flowers. I've had some sent down to the concierge, and some I've given to friends. So much money wasted when there are children who are dying of hunger and cold!"

She thought for a moment and then exclaimed, like a little girl playing at being a florist: "I can offer you lilies or roses—the irises have already faded. Take your choice."

"I'd like some roses."

She continued her little act: "Ah, I've got some lovely ones; very fragrant, dark pink ones. I'll let you have them cheap."

"That's the first time a woman has ever sent me flowers!"

"And what a woman, my angel! Remind me of your exact address.

You'll receive them within an hour. Goodbye for now."

Two hours later, she called back "Well, do you like your roses?"

"They haven't arrived, Marlene."

"What!? That's outrageous! I paid a messenger, and he came 'round to fetch them just after we'd spoken. He doesn't do his deliveries on foot, after all. I'm going to call that place up and tell them what I think of them!"

She hung up, much annoyed, and called me back almost immediately: "They've been delivered. Yours is the fifth floor, isn't it?"

"No, the third."

"God! I said the fifth! Call up those people on the fifth floor; they've been given the flowers. Don't let them keep them, I'm sure they don't deserve them."

I proceeded to call up everyone on the fifth floor. No one had received any flowers addressed to me. I reported this to Marlene, for whom the whole incident was becoming a veritable tempest in a teacup. Not so much because of the flowers, but because she simply could not admit that anyone could do their work badly.

"I told him to hand you the roses personally! It's incredible, to think that anyone could be so unconscientious! That's Paris for you."

"Marlene, those people are up to their neck at the moment! We are halfway between Christmas and New Year's Eve!"

"*Ach!* You see that I'm right to loathe these end-of-year festivities."

She calmed down, and ended by finding it funny. She whispered the words of Henri Salvador's song "Cherche la Rose," in that voice of hers which had remained so young, and remarked jokingly: "It has taken me a certain amount of time, but it is the first time that I've sung that for so appropriate a reason."

"I do like that song, Marlene."

"That doesn't surprise me, coming from you. A pretty poem, a bit mawkish, and there you go! No, I would have preferred you to have received the real roses. Anyway, it was the intention that counted. But you can forget your flowers, poor darling."

A few minutes later, one of the seventh-floor tenants brought down an enormous bouquet of dramatic long-stemmed crimson roses. As I knew the woman, though charming, to be a typical bourgeois scandal-monger, I decided to put on a little act and do some name-dropping. I confided that it was Marlene Dietrich who had sent them to me. My neighbor, as I had calculated she would, spread it all over Neuilly that I was "a nice young man, but such a mythomaniac!"

A few days later, I told Marlene the story.

"That's always how it is. It's only the people who really know me who are suspected of making things up. The others write whatever twaddle they like, and everyone believes them. If that shrew goes on calling you a liar, I will ring her up myself to confirm!"

I didn't let her. Today, I regret it. She would have really enjoyed it.

∞

"Marlene, they are showing Maximilian Schell's documentary on your life tonight on television."

"Eryk, I forbid you to watch it! I forbid you, do you hear? It's a horror. They have dubbed my voice."

"Are you going to watch it?

"Nein!" she snapped.

"Marlene, your name starts like a prayer and finishes like the lash of a whip," said Cocteau. Always the two opposite poles. I disobeyed her and watched the film. Once more, I understood her refusal. She repudiated the films previous to *The Blue Angel:* "I had nothing but walk-on parts. I would walk on stage and say that coffee was served. Come on! One doesn't call that acting!"

A valid argument as far as her fist appearances were concerned. But the films made after 1926 prove that Marlene Dietrich was already a well-known actress. She, however, wanted her career to start with von Sternberg, turning a blind eye to a past she no doubt thought less worthy. The myth did not yet exist, and therefore neither did she. Simple.

"I am sure you watched the documentary."

"Yes."

"Ach! But I had forbidden it! Very bad."

"Everything you have done is of interest to me, Marlene. I found the film very good."

"No, I did it for the money."

"A perfectly valid reason. That's what most people work for."

"It's useless to talk about me. The past is finished and done with. Why persist? It's my only source of income. They know it! That's why they won't leave me alone. They are nothing but a pack of vultures."

"You are a myth, Marlene, you have to accept it!"

"Ah, that's a stupid expression! I couldn't care less about the legend."

"Why spend so much energy defending it, then?"

"I don't defend it. I defend my privacy! It has nothing to do with my films. It's a different thing. I know why you like Schell's film: you are a *cinéphile!"*

She sounded quite fierce as she said this. My disobedience was to earn me a fortnight's respite from telephone calls.

∞

THERE WAS A GULF between us. But we had in common hours of distress soaked in whiskey and sleepless nights no drug could totally get the better of. The solitude we both had to endure made us worthy of each other. And was she perhaps amused by the gossip I sometimes passed on to her?

Nietzsche wrote that one can guess at people's suffering by their way of laughing. Marlene Dietrich's laugh still rings in my ears. It retained a youthful freshness, however evocative of the scent of faded illusions. Someone who drinks understands an alcoholic, someone who weeps understands the tears of another. We could speak openly to each other, for our respective solitude was painful enough for us to be able to listen to one another without passing judgment and, above all, without offering any false consolation.

Loneliness, once recognized, is understood and comfortable. Silences, the sound of breathing, are infinitely more important than words.

I think she was born lonely, as others are born dark-skinned or nearsighted. Fame, then old age, did the rest.

Chanel once admitted to Paul Morand: "It is my solitude that strengthened my character, which is by nature bad, that tamed my soul, which is naturally proud, and my body, which is strong."[8] So many points in common between two women who admired and respected each other and who were both too great to be rivals.

"Being alone has nothing to do with loneliness. One can easily find a remedy for the former; not for loneliness," Dietrich wrote. She was too cruelly lucid to think there was a cure for her malady. And to avoid those articulated puppets who would persuade you to believe the party is at its height when it is in fact over. "One must accept loneliness. After a while, one gets used to it, which doesn't mean that one is reconciled to it."[9]

I have often thought, after certain conversations, that her soul, nurtured on the great romantic texts, did not really seek to free itself of its *Welschmerz*—an untranslatable word, coined in Berlin, conveying the idea of a spiritual unease that seeps through you like a cold, grey rain, and which turned her into the unwilling daughter of the great poets she revered.

In his portrait of Garbo, Roland Barthes writes: "Her essence was gradually shrouded, buried under a plethora of sunglasses, picture hats and exiles, but it never suffered any alteration."[10] Dietrich had every form of courage, including that of disappearing when she was in full sunlight. Look at her face during one of those rare moments when her extraordinary self-control is suspended: it is the face of a Romanesque Virgin. It is the face of a hounded woman: hounded to the end by a pack of vultures, who hoisted cranes onto her balcony or disguised themselves as delivery men so as to surprise the old woman as she slept and thus break yet another pane of her universe.

At the end of a particularly long conversation, on one of those winter evenings when the light from the city seems to tell you that there will never be another summer, Marlene said to me gently, as though in a murmur, "Forgive me for having taken up so much of your time. I am so lonely."

"HALLO, THIS IS Marlene…"—as though that voice could have belonged to anyone else! She pronounced those last two syllables, accentuating them, like someone smoothing a long glove over their arm. She continued: "Have you taken the Temesta? Are you sleeping better?"

"No."

"It's true that, at your age, one doesn't take something to sleep, one takes some*one!*"

"I am incapable of sleeping with someone. After making love, I think bodies are stupid and have nothing more to say."

"Me too! Ugh! The French always make me laugh with their 'twin beds.' What hypocrisy, how French! If one sleeps in that sort of bed, it means one's alone, doesn't it? I prefer to say a 'single bed.'"

"Have you been happy, Marlene?"

"You do ask the strangest questions. Every extra day is one less day when one does not love.… But, sometimes, there is a miracle. Then, every day is a life in itself."

"But what is it to be 'happy'?"

"It is a state of bliss. Not attempting to understand. Divine foolishness. When I think about it, it is not the idea of death that's tragic. What makes life tragic is the fact that one cannot love all the time."

"To love, even for one day only, seems to me to be so difficult."

I think she was born lonely, as others are born dark-skinned or nearsighted.

"Listen to me: always refuse anything second-rate, for yourself, for your body. It is better to be alone than in bad company. One must make the choice."

"In the *Elegies,* Rilke says 'error kills.'"

"I didn't remember that, but he is right. He is always right, in fact. The trouble is that, for most people, their heart is no more than an organ.... You have a good voice. A father's voice. I am sure you use it like an actor."

"I don't want to be a father, and I never act!"

"Then you are not a Gemini, you are a Leo. You have the voice of a Leo, I am sure you are a Leo."

The way she would say "I am sure"—*je suis sûre*—will remain with me my whole life. She was certain of so many things and she said it often. I cannot describe the way in which her deep voice would fall on the "re" of *sûre.*

"Do you have a piano?"

"Er, yes, an old Pleyel ... but it is out of tune."

"A house without a piano is like a city without a brothel. Do you play it?"

"A little, but very badly."

"All well-bred young people play the piano."

"I am not a well-bred young man! I would hate that!"

"Nonsense.... You are being impertinent.... But, as a matter of fact, you are right. Good night!"

∞

IN THE COURSE of more than three years' almost uninterrupted conversations, of confidences she stifled like sobs, Marlene never uttered the words "old age." Others—often younger than herself—were considered "old." But not Marlene ... she was untouched by this temporal settling of scores. From among the multitude of her memories, she had kept a firm hold on that stubbornness which was hers by fate.

Sometimes, to extricate herself from some minor difficulty—a sentence to which she could not find the proper ending, a word that escaped her—she would say, "What can I do about it, I am tired." All the injuries of time were contained in the word "tired." We both knew it.

Her sense of the mysterious, her intimate acquaintance with ambiguity, became increasingly more refined. She was always ready to spurt out a reply, a justification: "Why go out? I am perfectly content at home." "See Paris? I know it so well...."

One would no doubt be content to grow old if the passing years rendered one insensible to grief. But the heart does not abandon us. It describes an inverted spiral within us, growing inescapably closer to a point which grows increasingly blacker. A great actress, another public idol, who, unlike Dietrich, was not averse to pronouncing certain words, once said to me, "I am happy to be an old woman. Old age has given me serenity, the feeling of having done my duty." This woman put the same determination into avoiding the myth of Faust as Marlene did into braving it.

Dietrich's fits of temper, her excesses, were often due to her youthful temperament. Her minor rebellions, her sudden changes of mood, were more characteristic of a capricious child than of an old woman. Aging—a word that recurs incessantly in women's magazines and on which expensive private clinics thrive....

The last years of her life lacked light. She would have needed an entirely new world, the salutary shock of some love, of God's presence, of some culture radically foreign to her, to force her out of her prison. All that might have helped her say: "I am ninety." The revolutionary change of finally living without a mask. For her, fear was not merely limited to the coquetry of a star; it was fundamentally the loss of a world which was escaping her like sand sliding through a clenched fist. By abolishing all ordinary rules, she could create the illusion of still dominating the universe.

Old age is like love: it only gives you what you bring to it. Marlene brought nothing to it. She created her own system of royalty. As good a way as any other of bearing what remained to her of life.

∞

"Is being beautiful a handicap?"

"I have never considered beauty to be my profession, unlike many other actresses. It was necessary to be beautiful to play the parts I was given, and I was so. But there are a great many ugly actresses who have had successful careers. Beauty comes from within. If there is nothing to make your eyes shine, the camera won't see you. Real beauty is inside. Or else it is prettiness, or sexual attraction, but that has nothing to do with beauty. As I see it, the real handicap is being famous."

"Being famous? But why choose a career in which, after all, the principal aim is to be famous?"

"Because when you are a student at drama school, you don't know what's in store for you. You study your texts, and that's all. When and if celebrity does come, it paralyzes you. I have seldom recognized the woman the press used to write about. And then, actors are often hopeless artists. Apart from a few great exceptions, one should avoid them."

"Why?"

"Don't try and make me talk about Hollywood—I can see that that's what you are trying to make me do! It's a world in which it is difficult to keep one's dignity, to find the strength to be dignified. I had German roots, a family, and that is what gave me the strength That's why I survived. For me, the only thing that counts is the work. And if it is not good, start again! But, obviously, the more of a perfectionist you are, the more demanding, the more they think you are a damned nuisance. The failures, they never leave you in peace! And yet, perfection is so simple. Look at a Cézanne, a Balenciaga—no fuss, no complication. Everything is simplified. And simplification is close to perfection, whether in life or in art. To simplify a problem is not necessarily to solve it. But it does mean concentrating all one's energy on finding a solution."

Photo © John Engstead

"I have never considered beauty to be my profession, unlike many other actresses."

"You do seem to me to be demanding, I agree, but not a 'damned nuisance.'"

"That's because you yourself are such a damned nuisance! I have my ups and downs. I show you my ups. That's what is meant by good manners."

∞

Hollywood was rarely a subject of conversation. That was a veiled but persistent convention between us. At the time I had only a vague idea of what this refusal might mean. I took it, I think, for dry nostalgia for an era of white fox furs, limousines, and lovers in tuxedos that would never again return. No doubt there were more complicated reasons, as there often are for things that seem obvious. Even if Dietrich had enough clout not to be crushed by the dictates of the studios, as Louise Brooks and Frances Farmer were, she loathed speaking of her Hollywood years, just as the victim of a rape might loathe having to keep up a calm facade before a blasé, misogynistic police inspector.

Hollywood, I came to understand, symbolized for her not only nostalgia for her vanished youth, but violation and even abject misery. I sometimes would discover photos of her, awash in acres of satin at premieres and balls. She would claim, the next day, that Hollywood for her had been a factory—up at 4 AM, in bed by 9:00 at the latest. No time for dreams, and above all, none whatsoever for those vulgar amusements, those bacchanals à la F. Scott Fitzgerald, without the Great Gatsby. It wasn't *her* in the photo, she would hiss; I had made an absurd mistake; I hadn't looked properly; she had never met that idiotic Jean Harlow; I must have mixed her up with the *terrible* Lombard who had "stolen" her eyelashes without being able, of course, to kidnap her glamour. Lombard, who had that ridiculous fringe on her forehead to "hide a scar."

"Are you sure?"

"Of course I'm sure.... At least, that's what I was told."

Of course, she'd *have* to have been told, since she had never gone to those parties....

I was able to collect over the years, however, a few fragments of Hollywood gossip without her realizing it. Was she aware how distant in time the things she evoked were? Perhaps. She always spoke of the film world with total disgust. When I seemed amazed at the depth of her disdain, she would rear like a frightened horse: "Why do you seem so surprised? Hollywood is Hollywood. Vulgarity was invented for those people!"

She would concede certain exceptions. Garbo wasn't vulgar, for example—too great. Katherine Hepburn was the queen of her personal pantheon: she was "too good for Hollywood." Talking of Hepburn inevitably lead to Spencer Tracy. "We kept impossible hours during the filming of *Judgment in Nuremberg*. Mr. Tracy was difficult, but he was a genius, so everyone accepted the hours he wanted."

I replied that genius did not justify caprice, and that it could also walk hand-in-hand with humility.

She shut me up fast: "What do *you* know about it? See a lot of geniuses, do you?"

As for Crawford, she was one more "terrible woman, so ordinary, sweetheart, so low class. *Aaahh!*" And that drawn-out sigh unfurled all the disdain in the world.

Yet for Marlene, Christina Crawford's book *Mommy Dearest* was an absolute abomination. Sales of it should *immediately* be forbidden. Whether her story was true or not didn't concern Dietrich. "It just isn't done, and that's all."

"You know," she said once, "the people in silent films were so awful, they murdered Valentino."

"They murdered him?"

"Yes. The poor man was making tests for some film or other, complained of terrible abdominal pains, but was forced to go on working. He died of peritonitis almost immediately."

"But Marlene, you weren't there in the silent film days, so how do you know?"

"I was told."

I am not sure whether Marlene's accusation had any foundation, but what was vital to her was always to blacken Hollywood as much as she possibly could. One day, she sent me the French edition of her memoirs, in which—quite uncharacteristically—she wrote rather kindly about Mae West. Yet when I later asked a question about her, Marlene replied frostily: "I didn't know her. Just because we were members of the same studio doesn't mean we were friends."

"But you wrote . . ."

"I didn't know her."

That was that. There was no point in insisting.

One thing that made her *really* mad was the deification of James Dean. "I saw him once in the corridor of a theater. I said to myself, 'Is *that* James Dean?' He was small, ugly, hunched, with a potbelly and bowlegged. He seemed very dirty too, and kept digging his fingers into his nose. What a horrible little man! He had the good luck to die young and that's the only reason he's on every poster everywhere. If he had survived, he'd have had an even fatter belly, worn a wig, and be dead by now of AIDS."

Dietrich would not hear of any dissenting views about Dean. The world was simply crazy to admire him in any way. This suited me; I've never liked him.

"And then," she once said, "there was *that one* who gave venereal disease to everyone in Beverly Hills. If I told you her name, you'd be shocked." She told me her name, and I was.

And of another actor, supreme icon of virility on the screen, who revealed himself a zero in bed, she said, "Even with men he was hopeless! People used to call him 'The Great Illusion.'"

Dirty stories amused her. She told me some that would draw blushes from an entire barracks of soldiers. I don't intend to repeat them here. I have to admit, though, that I look at the screen with a different eye when "certain people" appear.

A friend of Dietrich's, to whom I spoke after her death about her hatred of Hollywood, told me, "What Marlene could never forgive them was that they categorized her for a time as box-office poison."

Part of the truth, perhaps—especially since Crawford was on the same list.

THERE IS NO END to the paradoxes that punctuated her existence. She hated talking about the movies—at least, as far as her own films were concerned. It was out of the question that I should broach the subject. If she decided to do so—which was very rare—she would do it while weighing every word, and speaking in the third person of the heroines she had played. It was a form of detachment rather than megalomania. A way of saying: "I have been that woman, but it was not myself."

She would talk about Josef von Sternberg—whose passage through her life had been of such importance—with avarice, with diffidence. As though by bringing him so often back to life, she had increased the debt she thought she owed him. No one knows what they were to each other. But their films remain—the only thing that concerns us.

Sternberg's work saw the dawn of Dietrich's career. The mutual love which emanates from it led her to her zenith. And to that beauty which is born of mystery.

Sternberg filmed Marlene as though she was his very breath, with a purity more violent than any grief. All their films are permeated with the vague nostalgia of a broken dream. Marlene smokes, alone in the corridor of the Shanghai Express. Sixty years later, she appears like an embodiment of that part of yourself that you reject. There is no key, no landmark. Only the image of that woman, like a crack between two worlds, sharpening our perceptions and revealing to us our common solitude.

All her biographers have dwelled on the complexity of their relationship and its effect on her image. As if one could find an explanation for sadomasochism in the mauve carnations stuck into an actress' brillantined hair.

Photo © Don English

Sternberg filmed Marlene as though she was his very breath.

Marlene transcended herself with each new role. Or perhaps she profaned herself. Her reflection gained in purity from role to role. As she progressed from the sequined tuxedo to the royal robe of the Empress of All Russia, her face gradually took on a sublime beauty. Almost empty, a Noh mask. Always extreme. Finally, just a crimson mouth and two barely visible, slanting eyebrows in a white, powdered, immobile face.

The public eventually tired of an adventure which seemed no longer to concern it. Their films grew into ritual confrontations in a language only they spoke or understood, from which the rest of the universe was excluded. An expensive perfume, at first bewitching, but which after a time becomes nauseating. The sun, at its meridian, was sinking into an eclipse, the present into the imperfect. They separated. But for both, the only concern was to be in endless flight.

"WHO ARE YOUR favorite painters, Marlene?"

"The only true painter of the century is Cézanne. In Cézanne, Matisse and Picasso are already foreshadowed. He is the father of all modern art. Mr. Von Sternberg often reminded me of Cézanne in the way he used light. He filmed me in black and white but his films gave the impression of being in color, so profound was his knowledge of light. Well, it is the same thing with Cézanne. A rather limited range of colors, and the light which shines out from behind the canvas. When you next go to London, go to the Courtauld Museum. There is a view of the lake of Annecy by Cézanne. Everything is there, the youthfulness, the vigorous brushstrokes, the mastery of the one holding the brush. . . ."

"One day, toward the end of this life, Matisse was showing a friend a sketch he had just finished. His friend asked him how much time he had taken to do it and Matisse replied: 'Three minutes and sixty years.'"

Photo © Anton Bruehl

Her face gradually took on a sublime beauty. Almost empty, a Noh mask.

"What a wonderful reply!"

"Edwige Feuillère told me one day how, when she was still a debutante actress, a very old member of the Comédie Française had told her that 'it was now, with all her experience of life, that she could have played a woman in love to perfection.'"

"Ah, yes, that's the greatest drama of an actor's life. Of all artists, they are the only ones who lose out on their art. Life takes away their youth while giving them talent. But it has never seemed to me that actors were also artists."

"The passing of time is even more tragic for dancers."

"Dancers, even those who have genius, are all idiots. Almost before they know how to walk they are being made to spend hours at the barre. Result: they never open a book!"

"Are there any roles you were never given but which you would have liked to act?"

"No. I have no regrets of any sort."

"If you had not been Marlene Dietrich, would you have wanted to dedicate yourself to some other form of art?"

"How do you expect me to know! I studied the violin. . . . But *everyone* knows how to play. Don't expect me to say: 'I should so much have liked to paint watercolors.' No, I tried to do what I had to do as well as possible. I think I succeeded, to a certain extent. One only attains perfection by polishing one's art like one polishes stone. Some have said about me that I gave the same recital for twenty years. But I polished my performance, I kept only its essential elements. There you are: if it were possible to define art, I'd say that it is what remains when one has taken everything away. . . . What I also liked in Cézanne was his mistrust of celebrity. He lived hidden away from sight, at Aix-en-Provence, on a small income—just enough to be independent. He sold very little. . . . The really great are like that."

"But someone like Cocteau was always looking for the limelight."

"Cocteau was very great in certain ways, but not in all. And moreover, it was the spotlights he was interested in above all, rather than the limelight."

Photo © Nicholas Muray

"If it were possible to define art, I'd say that it is what remains when one has taken everything away."

"I have often asked myself what an artist feels when he is separated from one of his works."

"But what does it matter? You are too romantic. You forget that artists have to pay their rent, like everyone else. And the sadness they feel when separating themselves from one of their works isn't necessarily that of a father who sees his child leave; it is rather that of a creator whose creation escapes him, who loses all control or power over it. Who is, therefore, laid open to criticism. If Giacometti's brother had not emptied the trash can every morning, we would now have practically none of Giacometti's works. He used to get rid of everything he didn't think was perfect. And he was a terribly strict judge."

"That, also, is a sign of greatness?"

"Yes. A real artist can be pleased by a work of his, never satisfied. Self-satisfied artists cease to be artists. They become merchants. There are, alas, only too many of them."

"Did you know Giacometti well?"

"Yes. I went out of my way to meet him. It's very rare that I do that. We met at the Deux-Magots. I talked to him about his sculpture, but he didn't listen. He just looked at me. I have never seen anyone who looked so sad! He lived on olives and alcohol. . . . Later, I went to his studio, in Montparnasse, not far from the Coupole, I think. . . . He was very ill, I think his sadness was a form of anguish at the thought that he wouldn't have the time to finish his work. . . ."

"In your opinion, what is it that makes people become painters, sculptors — or auto repairmen?"

"What a silly question! Cézanne was Cézanne because he couldn't be otherwise, and that's that."

A FEW DAYS AFTER the Rilke episode, I sent her a bunch of flowers to thank her for her gesture, which had really touched me. She took it very badly. Like all generous people, she hated being thanked. I do not believe that Dietrich put on a show of false generosity so as to "buy" people, as has sometimes been said. I know that she was a constant, almost pathological, gift-giver. But there was nothing she could expect to get from me. I did not belong to her social set, I was too far removed from her to interpret her gesture as anything other than a simple, genuine gift.

One day I asked her, "Marlene, do you think generosity is compatible with wealth?"

"Hmm. . . . It should be, yes. But it's seldom the case. What do you think rich people do to be so rich, my angel?"

"Er . . . I don't know."

"They keep their money! It's simple."

"You mean to say that all rich people are miserly?"

"Not all, but many of them."

"Why?"

"It's a form of fear rather than avariciousness, but the result is the same. Especially if they are *nouveaux riches*. You know, wealthy people are often very boring. Barbara Hutton was a crashing bore, and sadness personified. Those people tend to be very depressive: they have no real problems, apart from a total lack of identity. Nothing but a string of bank accounts. . . ."

"You must admit that not having an identity must be quite a problem."

"A problem invented by boredom, by inactivity. I have never been depressive, I worked too much. And then, at the time, one did not talk of 'depression' but of 'languor.' It was not at all fashionable. Nervous breakdowns only came into fashion in the Sixties, when everyone was doing well. It is an illness of rich countries. No one was depressive in the Warsaw ghetto."

"A journalist apparently asked Mother Teresa if she wept over the world and she replied: 'I don't have the time.'"

"There you are! That's it in a nutshell."

"Let's get back to being rich. . . ."

"Ah, yes. The only rich man I ever knew who was not a bore was

Onassis. If anyone knew how to organize his pleasure, it was he. He had the manners of a nabob, a caliph. . . . He was not at all dull either, which doesn't mean that he was intelligent. Most very successful men owe their success to cleverness rather than to real intelligence. Really intelligent men don't need to go into business. Randolph Hearst was an utter fool, but as cunning as a fox! When *Citizen Kane* came out, he went quite wild. He had, of course, recognized himself. All his press went for Orson Welles for absolutely all they were worth. But nothing could stop the film's being a triumphant success. Hearst's money could no more destroy Welles' genius than it had been able to endow Marion Davies with talent. Anyway, she stuttered. How can one act when one *s-s*-speaks *l-l*-like that?"

I found it difficult not to laugh out loud. She really was in fine form that night.

"But where's generosity, in all that?"

"Real generosity is invisible. One mustn't talk about it. As a quality, it is closely allied to modesty. Both cease to exist as soon as they are talked about. But, like nervous breakdowns, generosity is now all the fashion. Since it has become possible for sums given to charity to be tax deductible, it's amazing how kind people have become. Real generosity is always very discreet. All those social do's, all that 'charity business,' make me sick. All those idiots who pretend to take an interest in AIDS, or in the Somalians, to prove that they have a heart! Why don't they stay at home and just send in a check? Let them visit the hospitals. Only, no one would know anything about it, there would be no photographers! Oh God, what a world!"

"It is well known that you are a generous woman—I know it myself from personal experience."

"That doesn't mean anything. When one is well paid for one's work, it is obvious that one must redistribute a part of that money. People continue to think that I am rich. . . . Alas, I can no longer help anyone. I've spent enormous sums during my life. But I don't regret any of it. I have spoiled my family, my friends, I won't have been completely useless."

"Do you sometimes think you have been?"

"My dear, all sorts of things cross one's mind when one is alone all day long."

"Your friend Piaf had the reputation of being extremely generous, hadn't she?"

"One has to be very careful when talking about Piaf. It would take volumes to describe all her contradictions. It's true that she was very generous, but her generosity was limited to her entourage. It was a fear of solitude. She bought herself the presence of other people— of anyone, at whatever price. It was really awfully sad."

"What, then, is, generosity?"

"Money is only a secondary consideration. Being generous means being there at the right moment."

∞

Marlene took a dim view of Americans. She had spent decades in the United States and claimed to have the whole scope of American manners at her fingertips. The only Americans to find grace in her eyes were retired GIs, in whom she invested a number of qualities, no doubt as exaggerated as the psychological defects she detected in the rest of the population.

In 1958, she said to a journalist: "I believe there are all sorts of lonely people in America because the art of conversation is dead here. People do not tell each other their problems because they are afraid of censure. Instead, they go to an analyst. But that costs money. Analysts are not important anywhere but here. In other countries, people talk it out. In America, it seems to be wrong to do so."

I had copied out and sent her an extract from Alexis de Tocqueville's *De la Démocratie en Amérique (On Democracy in America):*

> I have seen men in America who enjoy the greatest liberty and
> highest education and whose condition is of the happiest. It
> seemed to me that their features were overcast as though by a

cloud. They appeared grave and sad to me, even when indulging in pleasure. The inhabitants of the United States cling to their worldly possessions as though they were assured of never dying; and are so anxious to seize any that may come within their grasp that one would think they were perpetually afraid of quitting this life before having been able to enjoy them. They clutch at every passing pleasure, but without embracing it, and soon let it escape, to pursue fresh delights.[11]

Marlene gloated over this passage. "It's exactly that! That chap understood it all!"

"But you nevertheless lived in America for a long time, didn't you?

"Because it was my place of work. Had my daughter wanted to return to Europe, I would have done so immediately. The Americans are like the Germans, only worse."

"You prefer Europe to the United States?"

"Naturally. One must be mad to live there all the time. For a long time I myself suffered from that particular type of madness, but now I have got over it, thank God."

"Why do you say 'one must be mad to live there'?"

"It's all in the words 'New World'—do you understand? What is new has no roots. Our castles have been standing for centuries but the prefabricated houses built in the Seventies have already got cracks in them."

"According to you, the USA is therefore more 'cracked' than Europe?"

"Go there, and you'll see what I mean! The Americans are remarkable organizers. And that's just their problem, they organize everything. Everything is planned, even orgasms!"

"Even orgasms?!"

"They live in a state of perpetual competition. And *for* competition. There's no time for anything else. One embarks on a love affair like one changes one's shirt. It's total hysteria. Men there have a horrifying idea of sex. For them, it is an activity that has nothing to do with one's emotions. And that feeling of urgency, of panic, ends up by castrating them. Real lovers are never American."

"You are blaming one country for an attitude which is, I think, common to most. Sex and love are, everywhere, becoming increasingly divorced from one another."

"Yes, but above all there! Americans have two brains, one in the usual place, and the other where the heart should be. They have no sentimental conscience. That's why their civilization is totally decadent. That childish side to them, with European touches, is nothing but exoticism. It's terrifying to think that the most powerful country in the world is in the hands of big children. Europeans have destinies, Americans have careers."

I laughed. "Aren't you being a bit hard?"

"Lucid, my dear, just lucid. You know, I've lived there long enough to get to know them well. One can take a whole lifetime discovering a European. But two months, at the most, is quite sufficient to get to know an American. Their outlook is so simple: Success—at whatever price, and by whatever means. And the first of these is an absence of feeling. Goethe wrote: 'If I had realized how many great literary works there were, I would never have attempted to write.' Only a European could have said that. In America one acts first, and thinks later."

"It's sometimes the best way of going about things."

"Well, yes, if you simply want to get something done quickly. But not if it's a question of a lasting civilization. They are in a state of perpetual mutability, but without ever managing to change fundamentally. That's their tragedy—ever since Benjamin Franklin. Only appearances count—it's all 'show-off.' Without social success, one doesn't count, even if you are the most fabulous person in the world. That's why they are so good at musicals. It's all in the decor—and it couldn't matter less if that collapses once the show is over."

"What you are saying sounds extraordinary! Do you mean to tell me that there are no genuine love affairs in the USA?"

"I hope there are, but I don't think so. Besides, they don't even feel the need."

"Why?"

"It's a waste of time, my angel! To dedicate oneself to anything other than one's own personal appearance or objectives makes for a reduction in productivity. You can have sexual relations with an American, but if that's the only thing that binds you to someone, you might as well go and bury yourself alive. Everything that is built on mere sex is ephemeral. Love is tremendously hard work; it lights you up, and brings you face-to-face with yourself. Bring an American face-to-face with himself and he will rarely forgive you."

"How do you mean?"

"It's simple. They get their own measure by comparing themselves to those they love. And, as they are not all idiots, it makes them dizzy. If you tear them away form their land of Oz, they become like rabid beasts!"

"Have you experienced this personally?"

"Yes. But I don't want to talk about it. However, to sum up, I'll just add that it would have been impossible for me to have had conversations like these with a young American."

"Why?"

"At the second telephone call, he would have asked me to recommend him for a screen test, or tried to interview me for *Vanity Fair*."

PARADOXICALLY, SHE USED to talk about Russia with unconditional, idealized love. She had sung there in the Sixties and had never, she said, encountered such respect for artists anywhere else. She would become quite lyrical as she recalled her Slavic memories; it moved me to hear her. She who shunned all "sentimentality" could, when she felt like it, be the most romantic person in the world.

"In your book, you talk about the 'Russian soul.' What is it, this Russian soul?"

"I have a Russian soul."

I smiled to myself. The only valid definition was one in which she was herself involved. "All right, but what is it?"

"It's giving all the time. One's time, one's money, everything."

"One can give everything?"

"The ideal would be to give everything without ever letting on. In any case, one must try to give everything. In the long run, it becomes a reflex."

"And the Russians are really like that?"

"Of course they are. They would dance on top of the tables and then throw themselves into the Volga while listening to "Le Temps du Muguet." Her voice became increasingly toneless. I sensed she was struggling against emotion.

She continued: "I have an almost mystical link with the Russians. There were a lot of them in Berlin, when I was young. They had taken refuge there after the revolution. I remember a magnificent-looking old man, who sold icons ... he was apparently a prince, or grand duke, I don't remember which. . . . And I loved their enthusiasm, their vigor, the way in which they could drink without losing consciousness. One toasts everyone, all day long! They are tragic children. Noel Coward used to say about me that I was 'a clown and a realist.' You have there a perfect definition of the Russian soul."

"You worked there?"

"I went there to sing. Artists are intensely respected there. They have a real standing, are really recognized. Not like here where they are treated like gypsies. Journalists ask you intelligent questions. They ask you who your favorite authors are, not who your favorite couturier is. . . . But it is true that many actresses are unfortunately more interested in couturiers than in writers. I remember in Moscow being intrigued by the fact that every spectator held a little white book in their hand, one eye glued to the book, and the other to me. I asked about this at the end of the show and was told it was a translation of my songs. Can you imagine 'The Laziest Gal in Town' in Cyrillic?"

"Rather unusual, I admit."

"When there is a theater close to a station, no train is allowed to pass during a show. I adored Konstantin Paustovsky. I had read all his works. His books stand out like the Romanesque cathedrals surrounded by Baroque churches. When I arrived in Moscow, I said I would like to meet him. I was told it was impossible, that he was dying, and so on and so forth. . . . That very evening, he was at the theater. He had left the clinic to come and see my performance. There is a photograph of that evening. . . . When I saw him climb up on stage, I knelt down at his feet. It's an idiotic photograph, but there is none I like more. He died a month later."

"Do you have other memories as moving as that one?"

"Everything is moving there. All those people who came to see me. . . . In Russia, the prices of theater tickets are reasonable on purpose, so that everyone may go and see beautiful things. Old women would climb on stage to give me three dahlias they had picked that morning in their gardens. I found that far more touching than all the orchids I have ever received. . . . A strange thing happened: I wanted to visit Chekhov's grave. I wandered for hours in a magnificent cemetery, without being able to find it. I asked various people where it was and they would say, 'It's there, quite near, at the end of that path.' And nothing! Perhaps, because I could not find it . . . I kept Chekhov within me, without being haunted by the memory of a grave."

"I'D LIKE TO TALK about the war, Marlene."

"Ah. How old did you say you were?"

"I was born more than twenty years after the Armistice."

"You know, in my book, I say: 'Don't talk about the war unless you took part in it.'"

"I am not talking about it. I would like *you* to tell me about it."

"The war—it is always the same story, over and over again, ever since the beginning of the world: a madman holds one country in his power and wants to take over the next."

"There are also the wars of religion."

"Leave God out of it! That's nothing but an excuse. Wars, all wars, are simply a matter of interest."

"But what about the Crusades?"

"What a wonderful example! Pretending they wanted to deliver the Holy Sepulcher, and all that nonsense, and then, when they got to Jerusalem, proclaiming themselves kings, princes, counts. Where does religion come into it? Rubbish—it was nothing but ambition!"

"And the Islamic wars?"

"Greed, always greed! Farmers always want to own the field of their next-door neighbor. Moreover, those countries are governed by madmen, by men who are sick."

"Let's get back to the last war . . . you took part in it."

"That's why the Germans hate me. When I went back there to give my show, they threw tomatoes and rotten eggs at me on the stage. I went on singing as though everything was normal. Then they said to themselves, 'She is one of us, we'll put up with her 'til the end.' But that doesn't mean that they've ever forgiven me."

"But why so much hatred? After so many years?"

"The Germans are tenacious. Don't forget that I became an American in 1939."

"But you left Germany before the Nazis came to power."

Ja, ja, ja. . . . But I refused to go back. They did everything they could to tempt me back. Goebbels wanted to turn me into the Egeria of the Third Reich. I would have made as much money as in Hollywood. Then they made the other one work . . . you know, that silly old fool. . . . She has turned over a new leaf now; she plays at being some sort of a Commandant Cousteau. Films exotic fish! Unreal, isn't it? You know, during the war, the Germans knew that I was at the front and had orders to shoot me down. To shoot at sight."

"What courage!"

"No, no, my angel, courage doesn't come into it. When one knew that pregnant women were being gassed, one did not think about oneself for long, one simply got on with things."

"People knew about it?"

"Naturally! One more reason for hating the Germans. We all knew it. All those people who lived near the camps and who saw the smoke rise up, and smelled it, do you really think they thought those were cakes being baked? I have always been very open about it: the Germans all knew."

"What you are saying there is very hard."

"And they, were they not hard? Don't believe the encyclopedias, everyone knew all about it."

"What was it like, the war?"

"You are being really stupid; you ask that just as though you were asking 'What is the Sistine Chapel like?' War is horrible, and fabulous. All those men, young, good-looking men, who came to hear me sing and who were killed three hours later. I was not a star, I was a pal of theirs. I ate out of a mess-tin. We used to laugh a lot at those stars who joined up so as to wear a uniform cut by Adrian. A bunch of funkers, those Hollywood actors. Except for Gable . . . but there was never any doubt about his courage. He wanted to die. He could not get over Carole Lombard's death. That was a different problem."

"But why do you say that it was fabulous?"

"Because it's in moments of danger, of crisis, that people show themselves as they really are. In ordinary life, you can't immediately tell who is the coward and who is the real man. At the front, you can no longer cheat."

"You are fascinated by war, aren't you?"

"What? You are completely mad! I like discipline. Soldiers. But war is shit. *Shit!*"

"If there was another war, would you adopt the same attitude?"

"Time has passed for me, sweetheart. And if another war were to break out, one wouldn't have the time to adopt anything at all. Too many horrible things have been invented now. One would simply explode before one knew where one was."

∞

"Whence comes that husky voice that speaks of broken hearts, that voice made somber by a myriad desires; and from what sea does that immortal siren rise who forever binds Ulysses to the mast of his ship?"   —Jean Cau

As I have already said, I have very few memories of Dietrich on stage. The little boy of eight who first saw her perform received an impression of sincerity. One cannot lie to a child. I could not understand a single word of the lady's songs but, inexplicably, I knew she was telling the truth. She was to be, in some way, an unconscious oracle that was to influence my whole life, making me detest all that was false or hollow.

I told her this one day and she laughed—at herself, but, above all, at me: "At last, someone who understands me!"

Later, I was to see some videotapes of excerpts of her shows and of the entire concert given in London in 1973, the only complete recording of any of Dietrich's performances. A show she had wanted to be perfect. She felt the time was coming when she would have to hang up her sequined dress and she wanted to leave future genera tions some record of what she had given her audiences. She had hated the result and had prophesied: "They will probably show it again after my death. Prospects of a great success!"

I had bought the videotape of the show. She exclaimed, "You could at least have consulted me, couldn't you, before buying that rubbish?"

"The video of your concert is on sale in all the shops, Marlene, and I like the result very much."

"Well, all right," she replied, in the sarcastic and abrupt tone she reserved for subjects she did not want to discuss, "but it's nothing to boast about. You must at least admit that the discovery of penicillin is of more importance than that damned rubbish at Drury Lane!"

On stage, she was like a figurehead, an emblem of total purity. The vestige of a world engulfed. The ultimate expression of a lost society. She was a living proof that one cannot be banished from one's dreams.

Dietrich adored the "Victory of Samothrace" in the Louvre. She saw her as the personification of ravaged womanhood and used to say of her, "There is more beauty in her than in all other statues because she does something. The others are idle."

She sang of grief in the same way that the statue might have. The Samothrace figure had opened her arms so often to embrace some wayward creature that they had broken off. But she could still spread her wings, just wide enough to be able to fly away. And it mattered little if she were to fall back to the ground. The main thing was that she should do so far from human sight.

Her songs were like the pungent smoke that hangs in the air, threatening and fantastic, after a huge forest fire. The smoke recalls what it was like *before* the fire. The glowing embers are even more dangerous than the flames.

The Japanese place great value on broken ceramics. Much more so than on those which are intact, for the broken piece is often repaired with rivulets of liquid gold. Beauty rising out of the ashes. Dietrich's art seems to proclaim: "Nothing must be as it is so that everything may remain as it was."

Natalie Clifford-Barney once said, "The most beautiful of all creations is that of time, the time one spends creating oneself." Dietrich had devoted much time to creating herself, with much success. The stage was her vital element, her universal element. There, she was her own mistress, her own stage manager, free to exploit to the utmost the lessons she had learned in her years in film.

She held her profound knowledge of lighting directly from von Sternberg. Though claiming to "destroy the myth," she in fact never failed to strengthen the illusion when performing to her audience. She was like a star, crowned with the halo of the years, and yet ageless.

Jean-Pierre Aumont was impressed by her perfectionism. During a rehearsal for her 1962 show at the Olympia, he watched her give all the electricians technical lessons: "I want some pink, a franker No. 14 for my cheekbones.... Intensify the lighting.... The spotlights on the side are too strong. Lower them." With her genius for light, her sequin-covered body rising out of the white foam, and above all that voice, *the* voice, she was no longer just Galatea, but both Galatea and Pygmalion.

Her real debut as a singer dates back to 1953. The extant recordings of the recital are not very good. The voice is stiff, almost timorous. It is not yet aware of its potential. The true *diseuse* did not make her appearance until 1957, when Burt Bacharach entered her life as an artist. He was exactly half her age and was to play the same role in her singing career that Sternberg had played thirty years earlier in her acting career.

"This was the greatest upheaval of my professional life. After having been catapulted into a world of which I was totally ignorant, I had at last found a master. B.B. took my number to pieces, entirely restructured it, and turned it into a real show."[12]

He did better still. He literally taught her how to bring out everything she had in her to give. Her voice became more assured, more flexible. The orchestrations became so sophisticated as to go beyond sophistication. Enveloped in a music which was like the sound of pearls dropping into water, Dietrich forged a style out of her despair and dared to sing. Bacharach coaxed from her the phrasing that was intrinsically hers. She accented each word and her defects were turned inexplicably into qualities. Her voice, albeit with its very limited register—hardly more than an octave and a half—could be of steel or of velvet. But black velvet, never sweet like honey. A somber hue to suit the intimate tragedies of which Dietrich sang.

Marlene Dietrich's voice was of the night. Kenneth Tynan wrote: "Her songs soothe grief. Her voice tells you that, whatever hell you inhabit, she has been there before you and survived."

Her voice has gone. I am left her voice.

She used to sing Harold Arlen's "One for My Baby, One for the Road" in a tone like the night, like three o'clock in the morning, when the last revelers have dragged themselves to bed and there is still far to go before the break of dawn. The no-man's land of time. Loneliness creeps into the final "lonesome" like a snake into its hole.

A number of artists have tried their hand at singing "Accustomed to Her Face": Lena Horne, Frank Sinatra, Dean Martin, to name a few. In my opinion, none can rival Dietrich in this song. I have played and replayed her recording. As one listens to it, one realizes to what extent a "cozy" happiness, a truly gentle way of life innocent of all insanity, has become part of her existence. But what Dietrich emphasizes—and this is altogether ignored by the others—is that nothing will ever again be the same if this happiness disappears. Dietrich's interpretation is permeated with an ever-present sense of tragedy that eclipses the overly "healthy" vocal beauty of other interpretations. No one has ever surpassed Dietrich in her mastery of innuendo, whether tragic, equivocal, or suggestive.

The whole climate of "When the World Was Young" is given us in its opening lines, with a dramatic sense worthy of the Greeks:

> *It is not by chance, I happen to be*
> *A femme fatale, the toast of Paris.*
> *For over the talk, the chatter and the smoke,*
> *I'm good for a laugh, a drink, and a joke.*

One weeps with the narrator, who could so well have succeeded but who failed in everything, with such determination and then with such resignation. When she says: "Oh, the apple trees...," the whole lost paradise of illusions is contained in those four words. Even the "Oh" encompasses all the apple trees in the world which will never again blossom.

With her songs, she has left us the illusion of disillusion. She sings "Where Have All the Flowers Gone?" with the burning certitude that if men go to war again, this time it will be terrible, infinitely more terrible than were the two other wars she lived through. Kenneth Tynan notes: "She knows where all the flowers went—buried in the mud of

Photo © Nicholas Muray

"It is not by chance, I happen to be a femme fatale, the toast of Paris. . . ."

Passchendaele, blasted to ash at Hiroshima, napalmed to a crisp in Vietnam." On the phrase "When will they ever learn?" she flings out "when" with an utter disregard for melody, as though she were pressing a finger on our bad conscience and on that reassuring faculty of amnesia we all have.

In "Warum," she stills her tears to mock the man she is leaving, crying out: "Tomorrow, I shall laugh in other arms." Anyone who has ever experienced the agony of separation will realize, hearing this pathetic cry, that no arms will ever have the power to console her for those she is leaving. "One only has one chance in love, only one," she used to say to me. Listening to her songs had been enough to make me understand this.

"I Wish You Love" is total renunciation. "Now it's time to let you be." She had led her child on to the farthest frontiers of her abilities. Now, it is up to him to make his own way. But the maternal prayer is omnipresent. Because she so wishes it, there will always be lemonade on hand to quench a passing thirst for tenderness, and always a refuge against life's storms. Nevertheless, her part is played and she knows it. Pride, born of duty well done, vies with melancholy. One senses the terrible question that must have haunted Dietrich: "To whom shall I now devote myself?"

Tynan again: "She shows herself to the audience like the Host to the congregation."[13] A number of people have confirmed this to me: during Dietrich's performances, no one dared stir from their seat. The illusion was too perfect. To scratch one's nose would have destroyed the moment.

In his diary, Matthieu Galey gives a cruel description of Dietrich's farewell to Paris: "She advances, taking the cautious little steps of an elderly American woman suffering from rheumatism." He nevertheless recognized that "when her voice gushed forth, the emotion was intact."[14] He noted the fascination she claimed from her public: "At the end, the audience wanted to touch her, as though she were some sort of divine apparition." At the same time, Colette Godart wrote in *Le Monde:* "She appeared on stage, luxurious, smiling. One felt amazed, almost incredulous, when one realized what age she must be."[15]

A number of people have reproached Dietrich for the immutability of her song recital. But why change an interpretation that one is convinced has attained perfection?

"All that bullshit!" She told me once, "When I went to entertain the boys, during the war, I had little experience at it. I sang sometimes before thousands of GIs and the next day to only twelve. I learned little by little to give, to reach out to the audience. That is the secret, if there is a secret."

In *Le Jeu du Duende,* Frederico Garcia Lorca develops a theory on the mystery of perfection, which is in itself an excellent description of Dietrich's art:

> Turning to someone who was singing, Manuel Torres, a great Andalusian artist, cried out: "You've a voice, you know all about style and technique, but you'll never be a great artist: you've no *duende....* An old gypsy singer exclaimed one day, hearing someone play some bars of Bach: '*Olè!* What *duende* he has!' Those somber sounds, that baptism of black water, are the mystery, the roots that lie buried in the silt we are all familiar with, which we all ignore, but from which emerges the very substance of which Art is made.[16]

And Goethe defines *duende* as "a mysterious power we are all conscious of, but which no philosopher can explain."

What better approach could be found to Dietrich's singing than through these words: "somber sounds"—or, better still, "baptism of black water"—for her songs are like a baptism of fire, an immersion in ice, alternating cold and heat. A way of saying: "Let us not dwell on any situation, whether good or bad."

Dietrich carried these somber sounds within her like an open wound. She was a somber sound.

At the beginning of Sarah Bernhardt's career, Victor Hugo wrote: "No one knows where the enchantment comes from that emanates from her, but were we to discover its origin, it would doubtless cease to cast its spell over us." Sarah Bernhardt no doubt had *duende*. Maria Callas, Edith Piaf, Oum Kalsoum, Chaliapine all had it. And so did Dietrich.

Her show did, of course, have its detractors and was not always so enthusiastically acclaimed. Her great friend Noel Coward wrote in his private diary, after having seen her perform in Paris: "She has developed a hard brassy assurance and she belts out every song harshly, without finesse. All her aloof, almost lazy, glamour has been overlaid by a noisy 'Take-this and like-it' method which to me is disastrous. However, the public loved it."[19] And the public loved it long enough to prove that Noel Coward could sometimes be mistaken.

Dietrich was perfectly aware that her talent as a singer was not always recognized. She once scribbled, on a stage photograph of herself looking quite divinely beautiful, "Wouldn't it be wonderful if I could also sing?"

But there is no point in trying to define what is in itself undefinable. Marlene Dietrich was the first to laugh at theories about her "art." One day when we had been discussing this, she said, irritated by my admiration, "What is all this nonsense about? I would put my dress on, sing for an hour and a half, and go to bed. You make me think of all those critics and professors of theater, with all your talk about 'intentions' and all that psychological nonsense. All you had there was a woman who knew her job, arrived on time at the theater, and did her stuff. Don't try and read more into it!"

Forgive me, Marlene.

∞

"What does "being elegant" mean to you?"

"Elegance is a word one overuses a bit. It is, above all, a way of life. If the person who corresponds to this conception also wears her clothes well, then all is well."

"Elegance is part of you, it comes from within?"

"Yes, obviously, like beauty. Otherwise, it's simply a question of proportions. But we have already talked about all that!"

"Let's get back to sartorial elegance . . . whom do you consider to be the great masters?"

"Balenciaga, Chanel, Dior."

"In that order?"

"Oh, those three are all equally great, each in their own way."

"Whom did you personally like best?"

"Balenciaga, without a doubt. The first fitting with him corresponded to the fifth anywhere else. He was an extraordinary cutter. You know, the great creations of Mr. Balenciaga have something desperate about them. Very Spanish."

"Like some Goyas?"

"Yes, exactly! Goya is the bullfight without the gold. Inner violence, beauty, and death . . . well, you are going to think I am mad, but I have sometimes recognized all that in Mr. Balenciaga."

"It's fascinating, what you're saying."

"But I am a fascinating woman! Don't forget it!"

I loved those rare moments when Marlene was relaxed. When her mask would drop. During those instants, she could vie with any schoolgirl in appetite for life and *joie de vivre*. Dietrich stood aloof—ready, however, to rush in at a moment's notice. She went on:

"When I was a girl, in Berlin, it was Patou, Schiaparelli, and Poiret, the end of Poiret. It was all very ornate, the women looked like Austrian cribs, you know, all those fussy art-deco things—utter horror! A fan of mine once sent me a photograph to autograph in which I wear one of those horrors with a leopard-skin coat. The Apocalypse! Of course I wore them, because, at that age, one is an idiot. Later on, in Hollywood, I discovered Travis Benton; rather, we discovered each other. . . ."

"That is to say?"

"That is to say that we understood that, artistically, we could get a lot out of each other. A real encounter."

Photo © Laszlo Willinger

"Elegance is a word one overuses a bit. It is, above all, a way of life."

"He dressed you in all your American films?"

"In those of Mr. Sternberg. That's what counts. There have only been two great couturiers in Hollywood, Travis and Adrian."

"Adrian used to do Garbo's costumes, didn't he?"

I had just made my daily *faux pas,* uttering the name of the other divinity.

With the blandest insincerity, Marlene replied: "I don't know. He dressed everyone at Metro. He even managed to make that retired colonel of a Crawford sometimes look elegant. That shows you what talent he had. I can remember all those hours passed with Travis, discussing where to put a leather panel, a button. . . . "

"Do you still have all those dresses?"

"No, of course not. They belonged to the studios. Once the filming was over, they were confiscated. But it was of no importance, the work was finished."

"Later on, it was Jean-Louis who designed your stage wardrobe, wasn't it?"

"Absolutely! What a darling he was, that man. Is he still alive?"

"Yes, I think so."

"*Gott,* he must be at least 120! His dresses are a marvel. Precious spider's webs. He always dressed me for the stage. For my show at the Théâtre de L'Étoile, he created that great swan's feather cape I have always kept."

"You mentioned Chanel some time ago. . . . "

"Her coats and skirts are the perfect uniform for women who work a lot. They never go out of fashion, never lose their shape, even after eight hours in an airplane—not to be sneezed at! Chanel was a workaholic. She must have had a lot to forget. . . . She couldn't sew a handkerchief, but she cut straight on the mannequin, like a sculptor. . . . She invented it all. She was a very healthy person, a peasant. I always got the impression that she was made of thick, solid baked clay. She only had one defect: she couldn't stop talking. And sometimes it was perfect nonsense."

"What do you think of fashion nowadays?"

"Awful, just awful! That frightful creature, the big, fat, blond man, who makes his dresses out of that plastic stuff one uses to wrap roasts in.... Nobody dresses women any longer. They hide them. It's symptomatic of our epoch. Everything's poor."

"There's no *haute couture* left, then?"

"There are a few couturiers of the old school who carry on with some idea which they copy and recopy ad infinitum. For the time being, there is nothing. But it will come back."

"Why do you say that?"

"Because it's an absolute necessity! One can't always live surrounded by ugly things."

"AND WHAT IF we were to talk about friendship, Marlene?"

"If you want.... Friendship is a very beautiful thing. It's sacred. I've had the luck to have friends who were great men. Very great men."

"Could you define friendship?"

"No. Not really. It's like trying to define Cézanne. One doesn't immediately understand, but one receives."

"But you must also give, mustn't you?"

"Yes, naturally. Life is really nothing more than a string of exchanges. Without that, it is nothing but a matter of interest. And if one lives only for interest one might as well bury oneself alive at once."

"Do you make a great distinction between love and friendship?"

"Friendship is purer. It is also as hard to build up as love. But easier to keep. In love, one wants the other's good, but also, a little, one's own. Not in friendship. My friends who have betrayed me, I have killed them in my mind. They are dead inside me. Even if they are still alive. But that doesn't mean that love is less important! Not at all. It's just that these are two distinct spheres. One struggles less in friendship. Love, love is a rocket, a racing car. One must be on the alert, keep up the maximum speed, do you understand? Friendship is, how shall I put it—the spare wheel."

"Isn't it rather belittling, this idea of a spare wheel?"

"Not at all! Just try setting out on a journey without one. You're likely to regret it in no time."

"Byron used to say that 'friendship was love without wings.' What do you think of this definition of his?"

"*Mmmmm . . . ja. . . .* A nice phrase. But which doesn't mean much. Like many of Byron's phrases."

"And when friendship turns into love?"

"Ah, that's another question. But it's better to start love by love. To discover the body after the heart—that sometimes kills everything, doesn't it? One must discover both at the same time. It's monstrous to make love with someone for whom one only has a feeling of friendship. It's worse than feeling nothing at all. It isn't necessarily the beginning of love, and it's anyhow the end of the friendship. Love is love. And friendship is friendship."

"Didn't some of your friendships turn into love?"

"That's none of your business!"

"But, in the final analysis, which would you say is more important?

"Both are equally so. Which is more important, the heart or the lungs? Each has a specific mission, but both are essential. It's wonderful to hear a friend's voice on the telephone, but it's also wonderful not to return to an empty house. It's terrible to go home alone."

"And the opposite? Can love change into friendship?"

"I don't think so. Friendship after love is often a bastard, spurious love one shams through lack of courage. One knows too much about the other one, but one can't make oneself break with them. Utter misery! One shouldn't mix things up. The scars are too different. You know, sweet-and-sour dishes are not my strong point."

"You've had friends you preferred to others?"

"I don't have a Geiger counter in my heart. Hemingway I miss as much as I did the first day. I've been offered a fortune to publish our correspondence. I'd rather die. Noel Coward also. We were on the same wavelength. . . ."

∞

OF ALL OF Dietrich's many images, the most genuine is that of the housewife. That intangible, dreamlike creature was as much at ease standing in front of a stove as she was encompassed within the rose-colored walls of her dressing room. I have heard her talk of dishes, spices, and flavors with the earthy sensuality exclusively reserved to this realm. Steaming dishes of food, waxed and polished furniture, blouses stiff with starch and smelling sweetly of lavender, all were of real importance to her, on a par with love and good books. On his return from Paris, where he had been staying in Marlene's flat, Noel Coward noted in his diary: "She was in a tremendously *hausfrau* mood, and washed everything in sight, including my hairbrush (which was quite clean)."[18]

When suffering from one of her attacks of real-false modesty, her talents as a housewife were the only ones she would willingly admit to. Some of her declarations would have caused even the the least feminist of women to shudder.

"One is more likely to keep a man by cooking him a good steak than by rubbing oneself all over with scented lotion."

"But Marlene, there are men who like scented lotion!"

"There's something wrong with them, then."

A friend of mine told me a story about Marlene. One evening in the Fifties, they were dining together at one of the great Parisian restaurants. Exquisitely draped in a pearl-colored satin dress, her gloved arms covered in emeralds, beautiful as a dyad, Marlene had seized some cutlery she thought looked dirty and sailed off with it to the kitchen—from which she emerged some minutes later, triumphant, her gloves and emeralds covered in soapsuds, but with impeccably clean knives.

On another occasion, she invited some friends over to eat crayfish. She never sat down for a moment, and never got around to eating a single mouthful herself. Armed with a bucket of lemon-flavored water, she rushed from one guest to the other, giving a good scrub-down to anyone unlucky enough to have a momentarily disengaged hand.

She would at times pretend to hate German cooking, arguing that it was heavy and indigestible; but, soon after, she would send me some of that horrible liver salami she loved, of which her fans in Berlin sent her regular supplies. I tasted it once—and promptly threw the rest away. It was really dreadful. I think that was one of the few times I ever lied to her.

She expressed surprise at the number of new cookbooks which were constantly being published: "No one reads them! It's like the Pléiade collection. One puts them into one's library, and all the dishes come from a caterer's. And all that to impress one's guests. What a world!"

She continued to take an interest in all forms of household activity, one more way of remaining alive.

"On Sunday, I watched the cookery program on television. Those people have never cooked in their lives! One can't make meat stock on an electric stove and in so little time. One should write to them. It's a positive crime!"

"Don't exaggerate, Marlene!"

"I am not exaggerating! Imagine an inexperienced young bride trying to follow one of those recipes. She'll simply make a mess of it and wind up having her first quarrel with her husband. It's very serious. I forbid you to laugh, it's *very* serious!"

She, who so disliked talking about her professional successes, would not hesitate to declare: "I make the best cassoulet in the world!" She often talked about food, very often and at great length and with positive delight. "A well-cooked, nicely crisp schnitzel makes up for a lot...."

She knew that if her gustatory delight were to disappear, it would mean weighing one more of life's anchors.

Photo © The Kobal Collection, New York

"Retire from the scene. It is the most beautiful form of fidelity when one has experienced the best."

A year before her death, Marlene said to me: "The tragedy of today's couples is the washing machine."

"How's that?"

"We have lost the whole ritual of the river, of nature, of love—all that, simply so as to gain time. To gain so little and lose so much! How very sad."

∞

"What did you say was the name of that Portuguese poet you were telling me about?"

"Pessoa. Fernando Pessoa."

"Ah, yes . . . you sent me his book, but it's in very small print and my sight is getting weaker."

I read her one of the poems in *Letters to the Bride,* the only book of Pessoa's I had with me.

"Ja, ja, ja. . . . He is having a rough time, isn't he? When in love, one of the two suffers and the other is bored; it is better to part."

"It isn't always easy to leave, Marlene."

"Isn't it? It is, however more honest. But it's true that honesty and love . . . *hmmm.* No, one really has to leave. Retire from the scene. It is the most beautiful form of fidelity when one has experienced the best. One mustn't wait until love smells of yesterday's stale cigarette ends. But one must have loved very much to know how to leave. That's why so many couples tear each other apart and remain together; they don't love each other enough. . . ."

I sense her profound melancholy, her intense weariness of life. She tries to escape but it catches up with her. Three or four people are still close to her. But when the door closes and she is left face-to-face with her past, face-to-face with the prison she has built for herself, whose walls grow thicker and thicker as the years go by, that prison poets and fools call "the legend," then the air must seem heavy as lead.

I want to draw her mind off her spleen, and talk to her about a show I have seen the day before at the Théâtre Hébertot. She exclaims, talking about the main actress: "She really is dreadful! How can one be so ugly? Now that Signoret is dead and Hepburn's chin trembles, there are no more actors left.... Oh, yes, there's Robert Redford. I could watch him simply filling in his tax form for hours on end."

I object, and defend the actress in question. She turns a deaf ear to what I have to say and continues her one-sided conversation: "I saw Gérard Philippe make his debut at Hébertot in 'Caligula.' He was fantastic."

I admit to her that Gérard Philippe is not my cup of tea. I have always found his recordings almost impossible to listen to.

"Who are you to dare say such a thing? He was a genius! Not someone like you, who spends his time following the sun on its course."

"I don't want to quarrel over an actor who's been dead for the past thirty years, Marlene. If you want a fight, find another subject!"

"Ach! Anyhow, there's no denying that he was absolutely sublime in that loony part. You can't understand because you don't as yet have all the keys to madness. Well, not all.... But don't despair, you're remarkably gifted!"

∞

FEW ARTISTS HAVE known such worldwide fame as Greta Garbo and Marlene Dietrich. No one knows what the very secretive Divine One thought of Dietrich. In his memoirs, Cecil Beaton mentions having accompanied Garbo on a visit to an antique dealer. The salesgirl, overcome with emotion, had stammered out: "Yes, indeed, Miss Dietrich, with pleasure, Miss Dietrich, goodbye, Miss Dietrich." According to Beaton, Garbo had exclaimed, on coming out of the shop: "She can't have looked at my legs!"

There are a great many stories that people continue to spread about them. Which are true? When I asked Marlene whether she had met

Garbo, she replied, with a groan, in the negative. With two such "sacred monsters" whatever truth there may be is always exaggerated. Perhaps they fought over the hapless John Gilbert, the silent screen actor whose squeaky voice disqualified him from the talkies and with whom they were both in love.

Legend has it that Marlene, while staying at Gilbert's one day, opened the front door to find herself nose-to-nose with the Divine One. Jean Negulesco claims in his memoirs that he invited them both to the same party where they talked all evening about the different virtues of hot water bottles and heating pads. Marlene denied this story: "How could one believe a man who made such appalling films?"

The most tender story about them is one in which Garbo, during a stroll in Central Park, bent down to admire a baby, only to realize later that its nurse was none other than Dietrich, out walking with one of her grandchildren. Marlene drilled into me so often that so many lies had been written about her that I can, of course, confirm none of these anecdotes.

One day, after seeing a film by John Waters, I told Marlene how horrified I had been by the Fellinian excess of the actor Divine. She didn't know him, but the idea that a fat man would dress up as a woman and act in a film filled her with horror. The photos and articles I sent her afterwards only confirmed what she felt: Divine was a threat to good taste, comparable in awfulness to Stéphanie de Monaco and the dresses of Jean-Paul Gaultier.

A few days later, Marlene, still obsessed with transvestitism, confided to me, "When I arrived in Hollywood, they wrote that I was "the new Garbo, the German Garbo, you know...." (silence) "They didn't look at my feet, I have tiny feet...." (another silence) "Garbo has feet like a man...." (prolonged silence) "What's more," Marlene went on, her voice dropping to a low, dark whisper, "I'm certain Garbo *is* a man!"

She no doubt wanted to forget that they had both appeared in Pabst's film *Die Freudlose Strasse ("The Joyless Street")*. Garbo, the debutante, had stolen the show from Asta Nielsen and had collapsed, fainting, into the arms of Marlene, then a mere extra.

Ten years later, in Hollywood, they were peers. Marlene may possibly also have harbored a slight grudge against Paramount executives, who, in their enthusiasm over the godsend this mysterious Nordic stranger was to them, had launched a publicity campaign acclaiming her as "The New Garbo"—a description that Dietrich the Unique may not have altogether appreciated.

Her friends say that Marlene Dietrich always spoke of MGM as "Garbo's studio." In 1937, movie theaters dubbed Dietrich, Crawford, Lombard, Garbo, and Hepburn "box-office poison," and those divinities found themselves in a perilous situation. After a period of unemployment, Marlene abandoned her "black widow" persona for that of a rowdy kid in *Destry Rides Again*, in which she played the part of a sort of Far-Western Lola-Lola, shedding both perversity and pounds—a change which was to give her career a new lease on life. From then on, she never departed from this role. "Shanghai Lily" had exchanged her cigarette holder for a Winchester.

Garbo, on the other hand, bungled her reconversion. After *Ninotchka*, in which her laugh smacked more of pain than of gaiety, she went totally astray in *A Two-Faced Woman*. Even Cukor's genius was unable to prevent the disaster and, with time, the Divine's funereal rendering of the "Tchika-Tchoka" was to look increasingly more like a *danse macabre*.

The war put an end to all exports of American films to Europe, where the majority of Garbo's public was to be found. She retired. For Garbo, the cinema was an affliction; for Marlene, it was an adventure with the attendant risks and pleasures. Despite her protestations, she had been at all the parties, whereas Garbo fled society, screening the fading beauty of her face with her hand.

Dietrich was the friend and solace of intellectuals and artists. Garbo loathed social chit-chat, and the Old Masters hanging on the walls of her New York apartment were representative more of business acumen than of aesthetic enthusiasm. In his correspondence, Jean Cocteau gave his own definition of the two women: "Marlene is a goddess, Garbo counts her linen."

There is an amateur film, shot in the Seventies with a Super-8 camera, of Garbo doing calisthenics on the terrace of her house in Klosters, Switzerland. One cannot help being overcome by a slight feeling of discomfort at the sight of this tall, angular figure.

In the same decade, Marlene was touring the world and emerging each evening from the froth-like waves of her swan-feather coat in front of a two-thousand-strong audience of adoring fans.

It is tragic irony that, after fifty years' retirement and right up until the very last days of her life, Garbo should still have been pursued by photographers in the streets of Manhattan and Paris. There are so many pictures of the Divine One, dressed like a man, holding up an umbrella to protect her much-lined face from the scrutiny. As though it were the price to pay for still being able to walk along the streets.

They both died on a spring afternoon, within two years of each other—Garbo first. In his book, Louis Bozon tells us how Charles Trenet sent Dietrich a telegram: "Garbo is dead, all my congratulations."[19] The old star's death was followed by revolting rumors of the sale of her ashes to the California cemetery that had bid the highest price—the last touching gesture of a niece who no doubt considered that the Impressionist paintings and seven-room apartment left her by her aunt were not enough.

Marlene, to whom I rather tactlessly repeated this story, was very shocked by it. After a moment's silence, she exclaimed: *"Gott,* I hope they won't do that to me."

"I am rereading all Rilke, Marlene. It's fabulous!"

"Of course, it's fabulous! I wouldn't waste my time sending you books that weren't fabulous. It's at your age that one must read them."

"Why?"

"To form your mind, damn it! Everything with you is in such a muddle."

"Is he really your literary god?"

"Yes. He has everything. Like Cézanne. Light, shade, love, death. And, above all, clarity."

"You never met him?"

"Oh, no, of course not. I was a child when he died. I would have been dumb and stupid, as I always am when I come face-to-face with someone I admire. What could he conceivably have said to such a dumb little clot?"

"Do you find nothing to criticize in his works?"

"Nothing. The problem was his private life...."

"Why?"

"He knew his own value, so he never devoted any time to love. He was too afraid of bungling a poem."

"Perhaps he never found the right person."

"He didn't really look! He was afraid. That's where he went wrong. Art for art's sake, when one is young, is amusing. But after forty, one can no longer count on art to keep one warm. I think he died young because of that. If he'd found someone, he would have lived longer and he would have left the world further treasures. Being alone, his source of inspiration dried up. He had to die. It's sad, isn't it?"

"So, apart form love, nothing really counts, Marlene?"

"That's right, my angel. When one gets on in life, one sees that there is really nothing else that's worth the trouble."

"Do you have other literary gods?"

"Goethe has been my great love. And Kant. And Josef Roth. Hamsun also. I can't work up an interest in contemporary German literature."

"And yet there are some great things: Handke, Böll...."

"Handke makes me want to die! It's so sinister! The trouble is that they've lost the *Hoch Deutsch*. They want to sound American. What an idea—abandoning such a culture for something so second-rate. It's suicide."

"And poetry?"

"It's difficult to like anyone after Rilke. I like Auden. I have always thought he was something of a lesser Rilke, but even that puts him on a far higher plane than the others. He also has clarity. I find modern poetry grotesque. Like men who wear braces. If I thought you wore braces, I would no longer call you up."

"You needn't worry, I don't wear them. And in France?"

"There are some giants, but they belong to the past. Apart from the great classics, nothing moves me now. Too much egocentricity. One builds a book up 'round a toothache. There's no more inspiration left, no more rhythm."

"And Proust?"

"Oh, ghastly! Does one still read Proust?"

"I should think so. I like Proust."

"Not really?! I already thought it old-fashioned when I was your age. It's awful, all that Countess this, and Baron that, and the tearooms...."

"It's not as simple as that. It is an extraordinarily fine analysis of human nature."

"Pooh, Proust is just an old bit of rubbish. Too many words. He's like a gravedigger, scratching away all over the place.... One really feels that he didn't love anyone."

"That's perhaps why he can see things with such detachment."

"Yes, but he also died young, with all those nasty illnesses. He looks like a barber's assistant with a cold, he's dreadful! And, on top of it all, he didn't like eating. Unhealthy! No, it's really the book of an old queer."

"Marlene, if you take all the old queers away, you'll be left with remarkably few literary giants!"

"Well, you can at least say that you've had the last word!"

∞

She didn't like hearing the word "exile" mentioned, did not want to consider herself one. But she was an exile, in her innermost being.

Once when Maximilian Schell was talking to her of this, she had brandished his *nostalgie littéraire* at him, it being her shield against self-pity whenever she felt it invading her.

In her memoirs, she had written: "My favorite book is Josef Roth's *Job,* but I have lost it.... Material goods have no meaning when one is an immigrant. One learns to make do with the indispensable."[20]

Marlene was not the type of person to be contented with half-measures. She polished the world and an admiring world accepted this. Her predicament was, of course, in no way comparable to that of those obliged to take desperate refuge on the third-class deck of some merchant ship, but it was, nonetheless, exile.

I contacted a friend in Berlin. It took him a year to find a German copy of *Job.* I was then finally able to send it to Dietrich. She said very little about it. Just a "thank you very much" scribbled on the back of a postcard. Was this book perhaps some little madeleine grown to a monstrous size in her solitude?

The postcard showed her biting into an apple. "To size the apple and the statue"—Ysé's words, in Paul Claudel's *Partage du Midi.* Ysé, a woman who also fled continually from everything, wearing a mask of dignity to hide her tearful eyes.

I had spoken to her about this photograph and what it conveyed to me. She had voiced her scorn with a *"Pfff..."* and I had said no more.

Sometimes, a confidence would burst forth, like a pink flower on a cactus. I called her on my return from a trip to Germany. She said, "How lucky you are to have gone home." I felt a pang of pity at these words, and thoughtlessly replied, "But, Marlene, there's nothing simpler. You must go back!"

"No."

"Why?"

"What would I do there? One should never revisit places one has known as a child. They have taken up too much of our dreams. They can no longer be seen by our adult eyes.... You mustn't let yourself be fooled by nostalgic pilgrimages. We only love places for what we live in them. With whom we live in them."

As though sensing my emotion, Dietrich resumed her customary tone and added: "I am hanging up. It's tennis time on television."

On another occasion, she was talking to me about German cooking, comparing two different kidney recipes, when she sighed, "I am an orphan, I have lost my native land."

Writing about Heine, whom she revered, she had said, "I consider his voluntary exile in France to be his finest pedestal."[21] When I quoted this passage to her, she declared: "I ought to have rewritten that passage. An exile is never voluntary. A departure may be, but not an exile; the reasons for an exile are more profound."

What reasons? What did she feel on installing herself in those magnificent hotels, invariably in temporary arrangements? About always playing at "leaving-and-returning"?

"But, watch out, you will wear yourself out at that sad game," Ysé often said.

You leave a country, your country, for reasons of work, or love; you leave your country because it is ruled by terror; you think it is too late, when it is simply too early. Marlene fostered her nostalgia by engraving old songs from Berlin on the vinyl of her records. She would say to me: "If you leave, don't forget to say 'wait for me,' or, better still, buy two tickets. Look on love as a whole, as an ultimate goal. Don't behave as though it were something experimental."

We were talking about our mutual experience of having been uprooted. I was telling her about my wanderings to and from Berlin, Brussels, and Barcelona. She warned me, "Make use of my experience to build yourself a nest. One isn't always young. Don't wait too long. It's too late earlier than one would think."

In *Around the World in 80 Days,* in which she had a small part, David Niven says to her, while looking for his valet, "I'm looking for my man." To which Dietrich replies, "So am I...."

You must leave things before they leave you, leave what is leaving you, go farther and farther away. Until you realize that you cannot forget your life, even under other skies. Her profound romanticism, which she concealed under the appearance of being a "practical woman," compelled her to leave everything rather than run the risk of disappointment.

When the curtain fell, Marlene went back to her point of departure. She chose to sleep in the Fridenaü quarter of Berlin, a few kilometers away from Schonenberg, her place of birth.

Human and material impermanence had come to an end. There were to be no more railway platforms; she was no more to scribble a hasty "I love you" at the bottom of her letters, no more to wave her hand from a window.

Paradise regained.

MARLENE GAVE ME a quick telephone call, just to tell me of a funny incident of which she seemed quite proud. Since early that morning, an unknown woman had been dialing her number by mistake. Thinking that she was talking to a clinic, the woman kept asking, more and more imperiously, to be put through to her dermatologist. After ten or twelve of these calls, to which Dietrich had replied in her most haughty Prussian tones, the woman had exclaimed in exasperation: "For goodness sake, tell me to whom I am speaking!" To which Marlene had replied, regally, "If I were really to tell you, you would never believe me."

"ARE YOU IN LOVE at the moment?"

"No."

"Are you having an affair with someone, then?"

"No, not even that."

"Ah. One should only have affairs with people if one's certain to spend the rest of one's life with them, or else if one is sure never to see them again."

"Do you think sex is important?"

"Yes, in the right conditions. If one does it by obligation. Then—"

"By obligation?"

"Well, not to lose the other."

"Why would you want to keep someone if you no longer want them?"

"Goodness, how young you are! Everybody is torn between the wish to love and be loved and that other wish, to escape."

"And if one expects something?"

"Expects something from someone? You really are quite touchingly naive. No. You can already consider yourself lucky if you expect someone."

"But what about happiness then?"

"The allegory of happiness is a blue sky, a pure, blue, cloudless sky. If you photograph that sky, you'll find that your film has recorded nothing. A blank. You are not afraid of vacuity?"

"Do you mean that happiness is vacuity?"

"Not always. Don't believe everything I say today. Today I am simply talking like a tired and melancholy woman. Happiness exists, but don't be too ambitious."

"Why?"

"Because you'll find yourself being caught up in a whirlwind."

"You must admit that there are worse fates than being whirled along upwards!"

"You really are the oddest creature. Goodbye."

∞

Dietrich probably cared little whether she was accepted or not, but she embodied a mixture of all-conquering élan and timid withdrawal. Her psychology, her writing, were indicative of an outstanding strength of will, but she needed to be led by the hand. She had once confessed: "I am incapable of doing anything if someone is not there to guide me." This man-eating lioness also admitted that "a simple shrug of the shoulders was sufficient to make her withdraw into her shell."

Dietrich's hard look formed part of her "emotional deficiencies." The panic she felt at having no one to guide her drove her to retreat into a shell. Really fragile beings often assume an appearance of authority to serve as a shield.

Marlene one day said to me: "All my life I have had to play at being both the man and the woman. It's tiring."

She would have liked to have had a shoulder to lean on, and I think she had really tried to find one. She needed to lean on someone else's strength in order to keep up her own. All the men she loved were essentially strong, reassuring. She used to say of von Sternberg: "He had every right, since he protected me." And of Burt Bacharach: "I only lived to sing and to please him."

She wanted to be both the master who commands, and the victim who endures. Even her femme fatale roles suggest the desire to be tamed or seduced. Her vulnerability, her weakness, was an ever-open wound, an unsatisfied but hidden need she had had to live with, burying it under her armor. At the end of a conversation in which she reminisced about the war, she declared: "No one is really strong. Everyone's afraid—some less so than others, that's all."

In her memoirs, she wrote: "I have never been sure of myself, neither in my films nor on stage. I am not really strong. Of course, I have strong convictions but I am as vulnerable as a newborn babe."[22]

One day I was complaining of my lack of willpower when confronted with life's difficulties. She said: "Strength is the privilege of imbeciles. What counts is one's self-control. That's what gives one confidence. Don't try and make yourself out to be stronger than you are."

"But why?"

"Because blind strength is a totally negative state! It's nothing but false virility. If you want to be truly strong, retain your sensibility. Real men are those who are capable of weeping."

∞

"Paris, which is the place most far removed from Paradise, is nevertheless the only place where it is good to despair."

—Cioran

"WHY DO YOU live in Paris?"

"Because it's a town I like. First of all, I'm left in peace here. In other places, famous people are treated with less consideration. And, you know, I've spoken French since I was five years old. . . . When the war broke out, in Berlin, I wasn't allowed to speak French. With the passing of time, I realize that that was my first unhappy love affair. . . . One dies many deaths in the course of a lifetime. . . . My first death was on that day. That evening, in bed, I spoke to myself in French. Later, much later, I came to Paris; I found this apartment from which I am talking to you. . . ."

"But why Paris in particular, why not anywhere else in France?"

"I think it's the town I know best. For me, it's the most beautiful town in the world. People of your generation can't understand what Paris meant to us. The 'City of Light,' that really meant something. Paris shed her light over the whole world. . . . Nowadays, things have become more mediocre. But Paris is nevertheless still unlike any other town. And, believe me, I've seen a lot of them. I have the reputation of having traveled all over the world. It's true, but you don't see anything on tour. You dump your gear in the theater, you rehearse; you get ready, you sing. The next day, you move to another town. That's not what one would call 'seeing the world.'

"In Paris, one can stroll about. It has the most beautiful boutiques in the world. Those great avenues, you know, they exist only in Paris. . . . And sitting on a terrace to drink a cup of coffee, that also is something you can only do in Paris. It's fun just looking at the people as they pass by, or gazing at the Arc de Triomphe. . . . I love the

Arc de Triomphe. I have a real passion for it, as though it were a human being. It is strong, upright, always there; in fact, the ideal man! During the war an aeroplane passed under it. I always think of that when I look at it.... On Armistice Day and on the twenty-fourth of July, they put a flag under the arch. All night the flag dances in the wind, like an enormous butterfly. It's wonderful, it makes one feel like crying."

"In your book you say that in Paris the light is blue."

"And so it is! Any photographer will tell you so. The light in Paris and the Ile-de-France is blue. As though one were looking through the bottom of a blue glass. The light in California is white; it lacks depth. The light in Germany is grey, a beautiful pearl-like grey, a rather washed-away grey ... but Paris has the most beautiful light in the world. It envelops you. I think that's why all the great creators have passed through Paris. Everything seems more beautiful here, doesn't it?"

"You really are completely in love with Paris! You see nothing to criticize in it, do you?"

"As far as the town is concerned, no, I don't. Though, of course, lots of people do just anything here, under the pretext that the label 'Paris' will make anything acceptable. I have some reservations as regards the Parisians. Fashionable circles, to begin with. Everything is more extreme in Paris—maliciousness, too, like everything else. Discrediting people is almost a national sport, making mischief.... But there are mean people everywhere. And then, in France, everything is an excuse for taking a holiday. Every weekend is lengthened by some public holiday. It's 'Saint-Something-or-Other,' or the Armistice, or this, or that— there's very little sense of duty here."

∞

DIETRICH'S LIFE WAS a patchwork in which all the ingenious fabrications circulated about her—or by her—have been worked. She carved a statue-like legend in keeping with her film roles and personas. As time passed, the clay mold turned into bronze, from which it became impossible for her to extricate herself. But would she even have wished to do so?

I think not. She became a living replica of her own image. When a bird has lived all its life in a cage, it does not dream of flying away even if the door of the cage is left open.

She spelled desire. All the films in which she avoided playing her established part as a predatory female were a failure. Her public would not allow her to disappoint them. She was expected to ruin men, not work to feed her child. Ordinary, everyday life is not always compatible with orgasm.

When Pasolini offered the lead of *Medea* to Maria Callas, he gave viewers the supreme frustration: Callas sings only a single note, merely lends her image to the role. The public was not convinced. The envelope was too powerful to be malleable. It was not her performance that was to blame, but viewers' perceptions of her.

During the Fifties, Marlene worked hard at polishing her song recital, as though it were a symphony. She immobilized her appearance. Time was brought to a standstill. Her stage costume remained unchanged for two decades, with one concession, in the first few years: the formal tuxedo she put on before the end of the second part of her performance. Theory-starved cinema historians have interpreted this as the badly digested impact made on her by photographs of her absent father.

Marlene loathed psychoanalysis. She called psychiatrists "brainwashers." One day, I asked her why she had for so many years liked wearing men's clothes.

"Oh, don't pester me with all that ambiguous stuff! It's simply that they creased less in a car and that they suited me." She was guarded about this aspect of her personality, but her androgyny was conscious, oriented. To quote Kenneth Tynan: "She has sex but no particular gender."

In *The Blue Angel,* Lola wears a top hat and a workman's cap. The

Photo © E. R. Richee

"Oh, don't pester me with all that ambiguous stuff! It's simply that [men's clothes] creased less in a car and that they suited me."

following year, in *Morocco,* Marlene sings "Quand l'Amour Meurt"—an insipid love song written for a man—in a black tuxedo, before kissing a woman on the mouth in exchange for a gardenia. She embodies the bisexuality at the heart of our collective subconscious: the feminine element in men, the masculine in women. She is the ultimate in sexual ambiguity. In a way, this was the ultimate abomination, in an era when every female star considered it her duty to appear covered in plumes and sequins, and when the studios would squash any rumors concerning the somewhat shaky heterosexuality of their more glamorous actors by publicizing their (imaginary) love affairs.

All the accessories of the elegant man—Ferragamo shoes, Dunhill ties, cufflinks from Cartier's—form part of the Dietrich mythology. The high-pitched voice of her début was to become soft, dark velvet. At the end of her life, Marlene was to declare, with patent insincerity, that the erotic effect she produced was totally independent of her will. I asked her: "Did you realize how much you excited people?"

"Me? Not at all."

But justification cannot be found in her subconscious, for the constancy with which she chose, again and again, the topcoats, the sailor or Cossack uniforms, and the wool men's suits she was to wear throughout her life.

Her Fifties song recitals were divided into two acts: in the first, she sang the "simple and sentimental" songs, as she herself described them, wearing a lamé dress; in the second, in which she interpreted standard masculine songs, such as "Accustomed to Her Face" and "Whoopee," she donned her tuxedo. Unlike other singers, Marlene did not change the gender of the pronouns: the "her" remains "her." She sang them "like a man." And declared, with perverse naiveté—or naive perversity—that the "first part was for the men, the second for the women."

When I asked her, "Why the distinction?" she had replied, "It's simple, my angel: the gentlemen want to see a beautiful woman in a beautiful dress; the ladies prefer the tail-coat."

"You therefore acknowledge that your show has a sexual impact?"

"Good gracious, it's an absolute obsession with you!"

With this strategy she had found the ideal way of asserting herself. No drag act now is without its "Dietrich." Her appearance was brilliantly effective in assimilating her to the "third sex." And her sartorial reality has become a dramatic reality. Or an everyday reality, which is practically the same thing

SHE, WHO KNEW all there was about the triumph of deception, whose femininity was strong enough to enable her to face the world of men on equal terms, never mastered her ego sufficiently to admit the existence of a will superior to her own. The closing lines of her memoirs are these: "Some can lay their burdens into the hand of God. I cannot, and I regret it."23

For her the only holy scriptures were the precepts of Kant. She used to tell me that she had lost her faith during the war, considering that a true God would not have allowed such massacres. I countered that to make God responsible for human conflicts was like making crude oil responsible for road accidents.

As her end approached, she moved still further away. Ten months before her death, she asked me — or, it would be more correct to say, she declared — that "God doesn't exist, of course."

"I believe in God, Marlene."

"You believe that something remains after death?"

"Yes."

She burst out laughing, an unpleasant, cynical laugh: "What a joke! Then, according to you, my husband, or my mother, or anybody else, may be floating over my head while I am talking to you?"

"It's no doubt less simplistic, but why not?"

"*Gott,* how can an intelligent young man believe such a thing. . . . There's something wrong with you."

"We each have our own opinion, Marlene."

"Be more of a man! God is a consolation! Valium before Valium was invented. A thought for when one will no longer need anything."

Her most tenacious ghosts kept her awake, but her steely character continued to master her grief. She tried to rise higher and higher, so as not to be overtaken by doubt, knowing that the end was drawing close. Her voice, on the telephone, was losing its miraculous freshness. She would hesitate over a word, a fact. I sometimes had the impression that she was talking from under ten feet of water. Her lucidity, her irony were intact but the strength to fight was abandoning her little by little.

Her apartment at 12 Avenue Montaigne had become some sort of internal exile from which the rumblings of the crowd sounded more and more vague. When one is famous, there always seems to be a crowd around, but in fact there is no one. The idea that after having belonged to everyone, she finally belonged only to herself must have terrified her. Her heritage of illusions was becoming too heavy.

I had sent her a book of spiritual philosophy, *The Prophet* by Kahlil Gibran, which she accepted, hissing like a serpent: "You must be very rich to have money to spend on such nonsense!" Always that refusal, that fleeing from any comfort, as though she wanted to settle the bill of an accomplished life without outside help.

Marlene took all the light to herself. She kept it. Did she perhaps see God as the ultimate rival?

∞

MARLENE WAS THE MOST contradictory person in the world. One day she would encourage me to smoke more, the next she would lecture me about how I was "murdering my lungs" with cigarettes.

Bizarre ideas sometimes came out of her mouth, pronounced with the certainty of an oracle. God knows, she was *certain* of things. She projected herself into the future with a military precision that astonished those who had lived less. Now, years later, I often see that she was right.

One Saturday morning, I went out to buy a paper and found the body of a small cat on the pavement. It was a little black-and-white cat, and it had probably been killed immediately by a car, because it had no visible wounds. I picked it up and put it in a cluster of tall yellow tulips. The thought of this small life cut short saddened me sufficiently for me to speak about it later with Marlene.

"Where is it now, that poor cat?"

"Probably in the tulips where I left it."

"You can't possibly leave it there!"

"What else can I do? I don't have a garden to bury it in, and the concierge will kill me if I put it in front of the building."

"I have an idea. . . ."

Every time Marlene pronounced this phrase, I imagined a grey cloud hovering threateningly above my head.

"Go and get it, and put it immediately in your freezer."

"What?!"

"Yes. The people of your *quartier* aren't the kind to abandon their animals. . . . A little cat can't walk far. She has a nametag, you told me. . . . Its masters must be looking for it. Go and get it at once and put it in the freezer. You can give it back to them later. The body mustn't be allowed to rot."

The wildest thing of all is that I agreed without hesitation. I wrapped the little cat in a plastic bag and put it in the refrigerator freezer. The afternoon unraveled without further incident. I had forgotten all about the cat. At about seven o'clock, a shrill, prolonged scream tore me from the television screen. I leaped up. My aunt, nearly speechless, appeared wrapped in her red flannel bathrobe. In a state of shock, but exhilarated by the dramatic possibilities of the situation, Aunt M. barred the door, crossing her arms like a suffragette. "Don't come one step further. . . . (silence) *There is a dead cat in my freezer!*"

Reassured, I sighed, "Oh, it's only that. . . . Yes, I know, I put it

Photo © the Kobal Collection, New York

She tried to rise higher and higher, so as not to be overtaken by doubt, knowing that the end was drawing close.

there." Which only made her scream again, even more shrilly.

The cat remained in the freezer for two days. My aunt, of course, told me to take it out, but I refused. As she was less adventurous than she would have liked to believe, she didn't dare do it herself. She preferred instead to do without ice cubes and wait for the cook's return on Monday morning.

Once again, Dietrich was right. On Monday, the Rumanians who lived in the second-floor apartment, worried by the disappearance of their cat, knocked on all the doors of the building, only to find their pet in my aunt's refrigerator.

I have often thought about this episode. Marlene Dietrich, who ate every kind of meat, who had collected furs her whole life without giving a moment's thought to "endangered species," nevertheless had worried about leaving the body of a cat on the pavement.

Was she trying to "move" me? That wasn't her style at all. Was it the fantasy of a capricious, lonely old woman? One explanation, perhaps. But the truth for me lies in the word that for ninety years had governed her line of conduct: dignity. We had to protect the animal because it "just wasn't done" to leave something dead outside.

The tiny abandoned cat was herself, whose days and nights must have been growing more and more anguished, for she was far too intelligent not to understand that life was abandoning her with discreet but audible steps, leaving her stricken and sometimes paranoid. The little cat was also me, who hadn't decided on any particular kind of life and who was doing little more than vegetating, which must have worried her. As she often said, "Who will shout at you when I'm no longer there to do it?"

The small dead cat was everything that obsessed her, everything that needed help and respect, even in death.

Dear Marlene, it was you who called me in tears when the Gulf War was declared. "Presidents make their decisions, sitting in their leather armchairs, but it's our boys who have to go out and get slaughtered. God, when will it ever, *ever* end?"

It has taken me time to understand this, but I can say it now:

Marlene was difficult, sometimes cruel, sometimes savage and unjust. But she had an enormous heart. And hiding her heart was a constant struggle. She knew that having a heart in the worlds she had to manage was just too dangerous.

February 1992. I have just returned from Deauville. It is a rainy winter day. I listen to the messages on the answering machine. A string of them. At the end of the tape, Marlene's weakened voice reverberates in the room: "Where on earth are you, you naughty boy?"

It is the last time that voice is to address me. I often listen to that cassette. It is now very worn out, and the sound has become tinny. I have not had a copy made. In the end, it is of little importance.

"Literary nostalgia," Marlene would have said to me.

Wednesday, May 6, 1992. Marlene Dietrich has died. Suddenly. I learned of her death on the radio, sitting in the same faded beige study in which I had spoken to her for the first time. It seemed like only yesterday. . . ,

I went out, wandered the streets until nightfall. The cherry trees had flowered early. I thought: How strange to choose so peaceful, so unremarkable, a day to die on.

I knew she had been old and ill. Everyone knew it. But she had lived through so much. She had become a historic monument in her own lifetime. And historic monuments do not die.

When Marlene was carried into the Church of the Madeleine, the notes of the "Marseillaise" rang out, stilted and banal, soon followed by those of "Lili Marlene." Duty and spangles. Your daughter was there, shrouded in a black veil. She walked before you, a straight,

Photo © Ted Reed

She knew that having a heart in the worlds she had to manage was just too dangerous.

dignified figure. Your silhouette, almost your bearing. Her presence struck me strangely, as though you yourself were present, a spectator at your own funeral. . . .

At the door of the church, a frail, almost childish, transvestite was weeping. He was dressed in ridiculous clothes, a hat with a veil. Anywhere else, he would have attracted ridicule. Not here. The arch of his eyebrows was beautifully drawn. You, always you, in *Blonde Venus,* in the scenes of misery—do you remember, it was because of this film that I first wrote to you. . . .

"And when I die, don't pay the preacher for speaking of my glory and my fame," you sang.

Not glory, dear Marlene.

Present were those who loved you. The others were in Cannes, for the film festival. "They" did not put themselves out, even though your face—that of Shanghai Lily—was on the festival poster that year. Your last fit of anger, I am told, for "they" had not sought your permission.

Rilke's "Flag" was read out loud. And also a verse from the Scriptures: "What can it serve a man if he gain the whole world and lose his own soul?"

Had you gained it or had you lost it, that soul in which you refused to believe?

"I want to be left in peace, I want to be alone," you used to say. You had now joined your unloved sister, the divine Swede, who had opened the door two years earlier.

Now, you no longer had to hide. The time of appeasement had come. At last. You sleep in a little cemetery in Berlin, close to your mother. It is like a garden, they say. . . .

There, there are no more embraces, no more departures, no more cameras. You are free.

On coming out of the church, I helped a very old lady down the steps. She told me, when thanking me, that she had been a fitter at Chanel and that "Mademoiselle always used to tell us to be very kind to Madame Dietrich, as she worked too hard."

You see, everything is for the best.
Have a good rest now.

∞

I COULD NOT TAKE IN the fact that Marlene was dead. A silent telephone does not necessarily portend death. The absence of an image, characteristic of our discussions, lent credibility to this non-being, this immateriality. For me, she could not be dead, just as she had never been alive in the broader sense of the word. I could not imagine her breathing or eating. I did not, however, deify her for all that. She was the embodiment of the Chorus, the Fatum.

Sixty years earlier, a correspondence with the Duse, for instance, would have seemed quite as extravagant but more concrete. The art of letter writing is governed by a code of *savoir vivre* that excludes all spontaneity.

The heart's murmurings are more easily confided to the telephone. Marlene used to take her time when speaking. But she did it without affectation, without any superfluity of polite phrases. That absence of the "Open, Sesame" of social passwords made our dialogues totally unlike ordinary conversations.

I did not situate her geographically, either in Paris or elsewhere. She was a voice from beyond the heavens. Or from beyond hell. And frequently, hers had been the voice of reason.

For me, she was the mobile image of an immobile eternity.

I attended her funeral as though I was a mere onlooker, a spectator. I spent the afternoon reading in the Luxembourg Gardens. It was a very hot day, almost summer.

I was untroubled. She would call me up again soon.

The weeks passed, quietly. The silence was becoming heavy.

At the end of August, I went to Chartres. Every time I left Paris, I used to send Marlene a postcard. Always the same idiotic message: "Even here, I think of you." Because I really did think about her. And

Photo © Don English

"I want to be left in peace, I want to be alone."

Photo © Don English

For me, she was the mobile image of an immobile eternity.

I did it, too, for the childish pleasure of writing her name on a piece of cardboard. It had become a game between us.

When I called her on my return, her words would always be: "And what was it like over there?" After that, she would comment on the postcard itself: "The cards you choose get uglier and uglier! How do you manage it? It should be forbidden to sell such horrors. Or the shopkeepers should be sued." We would then launch into a series of fierce indictments and she would often end up declaring: "Only you could make me laugh over such awful kitsch stuff!"

I took a card down from the shelf, happy to have found one that was especially hideous (cathedral towns seems to be particularly propitious for such postcards). I wrote my message, her address....

I can remember looking straight in front of me....

I understood.

Nevertheless, I mailed the card.

∞

As I WAS WRITING this book, in India, I came across the statue of Shiva Ardhnarishvara in the Madras Museum. Shiva Ardhnarishvara, the God-Goddess, a compound of Shiva, the father, and Parvati, the mother. The green patina on the bronze emphasizes the hollows and curves. The two poles within us all, the male and female elements that govern and counterbalance each other. The residue, the compendium of a thousand divine endeavors to obtain the perfect being.

While I was writing, I realized that Dietrich's true image was impressing itself upon me. And as it is the voice that first engraves itself on our memory, Marlene's voice, its tone, would come back to me like some mathematical threnody, in the way one solves an equation by an accumulation of data.

All our successive conversations pieced her together like a puzzle, like a bas-relief rescued from the sand by the strokes of an archeologist's brush. Her presence has never made itself felt so palpably, she has never been so much alive, as since her death.

That statue in Madras symbolized not androgyny, but total fulfillment, the instinct of the helianthus as it turns on its stem, following the sun on its course from morning until night.

Marlene was a statue. *The* statue.

She had paid the price, but she had become a living work of art. The process had taken time. There had been sketches and proofs, torn-up pages and alterations. It sometimes happens that the gently smiling stone angels guarding our cathedrals are gnawed away from within by a disease called granite rot. If steps are not taken to restore them, they soon, very soon, crumble into dust. Which only adds to their tragic beauty.

At the beginning of his *Portrait of Dorian Gray*, Oscar Wilde has Sir Henry say: "Each of us carries in himself a part of Heaven and of Hell." Marlene Dietrich managed, in an extraordinary way, to reconcile the two. Like the statue of Shiva Ardhnarishvara.

Blatantly disingenuous, yet utterly loyal. An utter bitch and a veritable empress, capable at one moment of haggling over the price of a pound of butter and, in the next, of sending a virtual stranger an engraved box from Cartier's. Capable of paying the hospital bill of a glazier's son, whose existence she had until then been totally unaware, and also of kicking up a fuss because her secretary had used her telephone or taken one of her stamps.

I often think about the almost operatic relationship we shared— the twenty-year-old drop-out and the immobilized Star of Stars. *Harold and Maude* rewritten by an invalid Cocteau. I would think about it, without analyzing it too deeply.

We had each been, from afar, the other's fallen angel. Each after his own fashion. I, in my fashion, by keeping her abreast of life, in touch with the hum of a great city whose streets she would never again tread, except in her imagination.

My colorless life may perhaps at times have seemed as tempting to her as forbidden fruit, and I a living regret. She wanted to hear no more about the world, considering she already knew enough. I was reluctant to venture out into it because I knew nothing about it.

My existence was like a large tract of fallow land or barren, scorched earth. It was amusing for her to plant a black rosebush or a white lilac in it.

Yin and yang, also a symbol of the ultimate synthesis. Yet I always come back to the statue. On the black screen, on the white page, no interaction of colors is possible.

Some months after Dietrich's death, the film historian Claude-Jean Philippe declared: "She is unassailable. She is beyond all that can be said or written about her."

"For thy sake I in love am grown."
—Katherine Philips (*Poems,* 1667)

Paris, Autumn 1995. *Liebe* Marlene: Early this morning, very early, I walked down Avenue Montaigne. The pavement was still wet from last night's rain. The air smelled fresh, and of black coffee. You'll be furious, but your plane trees have been pruned again! The branches have been whittled down and cover only the first two stories of your building. The early autumn light was a milky blue, and it all made me want to write to you and tell you what I have been doing.

It is now three years since you left Paris. Paris, which still continues to look like Baudelaire's wicked old lady, full of spleen. Only romantic foreigners can love Paris. Because they understand nothing about it. For my part, I think that the little that used to bind me to it has died, since your leaving. However, this is all nothing but "literary nostalgia," isn't it?

I have thought often of you during the last few years. I am still as obstinate as ever. I still suffer from the same idiotic stubbornness, but I do not fight it. After all, it did *you* no harm. You used to say to me,

"Better to be pigheaded than weak!" Knowing what one wants is, after all, a form of coherence. Being at peace with oneself.

Since your apartment has changed hands, a lot of books and articles, radio and television programs, have been devoted to you. I must admit I have never been able to recognize in them the woman I knew. But that is a compliment.

You'll remember that I grew up in a world of aging, panic-stricken actors, a world populated by masks of vanity and cruelty. I, myself, longed to be an actor for a long time. And then I abandoned the idea, like so many others. . . .

Moreover, you claimed that it was unworthy of a man to be an actor. I grew up hating and fascinated by the very idea of celebrity. And, anyhow, what is the point of being famous if one is deprived of love? The Koran says that all is perishable, save the face of God. . . . No one lays flowers on Sarah Bernhardt's grave any more. And, God knows, she too fought on until the bitter end. But we remember her name. "The magic itself disappears, only the magician remains."

You often said to me: "Learn from my mistakes so as not to make the same mistakes yourself. Before you know where you are, it is too late."

Love entered my life a few months after you left. The circumstances would take too long to relate here, but I am in love. It is indeed true that it is an extraordinary blessing to wake up beside someone you love.

You prepared me for all that, without realizing it. You used to tell me, with all the tact of a Panzer tank, that it was better that I should be alone, for I was not yet complete, I was too confused. "If love crosses your path, you will not even see it. Wait, it'll come." It has come.

"Now it's the time to let you be," you used to sing. . . . I have changed a lot. I still, at times, fall into an abyss of misery. But my happiness obliterates my anguish, like a wave erasing words etched in the sand.

Love has changed the despair we so often shared into trust and wonderment. It is a challenge. But you must risk all to win all. Nietzsche says that it is only those who are prepared to risk being burned who pass over to the other shore. Love gives everything.

You have been attributed quite an interminable list of lovers and mistresses by your biographers. So numerous, in fact, that I can't help asking myself how you ever found time to work, with so hectic a private life! In any case, the only thing that matters is that you loved them.

I think you must always have given full measure in love. And that is no doubt why so few understood you, why so many were afraid of you. Your very name, Marie-Magdalene, evokes total, unlimited love in the Scriptures. And even if God did not exist for you, you loved more, and better, than many a "religious" person.

The winter fashions are horrible. You have left me the courage of my prejudices. You had many of your own but, with time, I feel that you were right to have had them. Total tolerance is simply the indifference of the worldly. Ugliness seems really ugly to me. But beauty also seems very beautiful.

I felt terribly sad while trying to recall and write down our conversations together. I thought that I finally had something to say. I had a voice. You helped me find it. I kept asking myself if I had really understood you. If this book would be a betrayal. Have I indeed contributed something? I know you hated Proust, but he said: "To have been useful—a modest and a mad dream." It is not for me to say.

In spite of a few cloudy passages, everything was for the best between us, wasn't it? I haven't yet found time to visit you in Berlin. But, between you and me, that is a mere formality. I often listen to your records. Everything you wished for me has been granted. Thank you.

I must, however, end this letter now. I already know that it will either irritate you or make you smile, according to what mood you are in—it is so "sentimental."

At present, where you now are, you know many things. And since it appears that nothing comes to an end, it is possible that we may finally meet face-to-face one day, isn't it?

All summer they've been working on the Pont de l'Alma. And there have been horrible traffic jams on the Avenue Montaigne and the Rue François. But Stéphanie de Monaco has had nothing to do with it. I have made quite sure.

The price of stamps has gone up again. The elections have changed absolutely nothing in French politics. The world has been plunged into a vortex of violence and darkness. No one has any idea of what may happen. Like you, I fear the worst. But I keep hoping.

Thanks to you, I know that one can survive.

Take care.

I wish you love.

Songs of Marlene Dietrich

Cited in the text

Falling in Love Again
Allein in Eine Grosse Stadt
Illusions
One for My Baby, One for the Road
Accustomed to Her Face
When the World Was Young
Warum
I Wish You Love
Where Have All the Flowers Gone?
Look Me Over Closely
White Grass
Quand l'Amour Meurt
The Boys in the Back Room
Cherche la Rose
(All the above copyright © Famous Music Corporation)

The Laziest Gal in Town
(Copyright © Harms, Inc.)

Notes

1. Marlene Dietrich, *Dietrich* (New York: Grove Press, 1984), p. 249.
2. Marlene Dietrich, *Dietrich,* p. 21.
3. Marlene Dietrich, *Dietrich,* p. 22.
4. Quoted in Louis Bozon, *La Femme de ma Vie* (Paris: Michel Lafon, 1992), p. 78.
5. Courtesy *Figaro Magazine,* June 1988.
6. Marlene Dietrich, *Dietrich,* p. 249.
7. Marlene Dietrich, *Dietrich,* p. 150.
8. Paul Morand, *L'Allure de Chanel* (Paris: Hermann, 1977), p. 55.
9. Marlene Dietrich, *Dietrich,* p. 259.
10. Roland Barthes, *Mythologies* (Paris: Seuil, 1957), p. 71.
11. Alexis de Tocqueville, *De la Démocratie en Amérique* (Paris: Garnier-Flammarion, 1986), p. 54.
12. Marlene Dietrich, *Dietrich,* p. 232.
13. Quoted in *Dietrich,* p. 254.
14. Matthieu Galley, *Journal, Vol. 1* (Paris: Grasset, 1987), p. 492.
15. Courtesy *Studio Magazine,* June 1992.
16. Gabriel Garcia Lorca, *Oeuvres Completes* (Paris: Gallimard, La Pleiade, 1986), p. 921.
17. Noel Coward, *Diaries* (New York: MacMillan, 1982), p. 387.
18. Noel Coward, *Diaries,* p. 333.
19. Louis Bozon, *La Femme de Ma Vie,* p. 116.
20. Marlene Dietrich, *Dietrich,* p. 154.
21. Marlene Dietrich, *Marlene Dietrich Abecedaire* (Paris: Michel Lafon, 1988), p. 79.
22. Marlene Dietrich, *Dietrich,* p. 257.
23. Marlene Dietrich, *Dietrich,* p. 257.

Photo Credits

Cover photograph © Turnbridge, 1937, courtesy of the Kobal Collection, New York.

Page 2, photo © John Engstead, courtesy of the Kobal Collection, New York

Page 26, photographer unknown, from the author's personal collection.

Page 32, photographer unknown, from the author's personal collection.

Page 34, photo © Erwin Blumenfeld, courtesy of Kathleen Blumenfeld.

Page 38, photo © Laszlo Willinger, courtesy of the Kobal Collection, New York.

Page 40, photo © Milton Greene, from the Milton Greene Archives, courtesy of Joshua Greene.

Page 43, photo © François Gragnon, *Paris Match.*

Page 45, photo © Milton Greene, from the Milton Greene Archives, courtesy of Joshua Greene.

Page 446, photo © John Engstead, courtesy of Francine Watkins.

Page 60, photographer unknown, from the author's personal collection.

Page 64, photo © John Engstead, courtesy of the Kobal Collection, New York.

Page 69, photo © Don English, courtesy of the Kobal Collection, New York.

Page 71, photo © Anton Bruehl, courtesy of Anton Bruehl, Jr.

Page 73, photo © Nicholas Muray, courtesy of George Eastman House.

Page 89, photo © Nicholas Muray, courtesy of George Eastman House.

Page 94, photo © Laszlo Willinger, courtesy of the Kobal Collection, New York.

Page 100, photographer unknown, courtesy of the Kobal Collection, New York.

Page 116, photo © E. R. Richee, courtesy of the Kobal Collection, New York.

Page 121, photographer unknown, courtesy of the Kobal Collection, New York.

Page 124, photo © Ted Reed, courtesy of the Kobal Collection, New York.

Page 127, photo © Don English, courtesy of the Kobal Collection, New York.

Page 128, photo © Don English, courtesy of the Kobal Collection, New York.

HOUSTON PUBLIC LIBRARY

R01030 82616

FARCA   791
         .4302
         8
         D251H

HANUT, ERYK
    I WISH YOU LOVE : CON-
VERSATIONS WITH MARLENE
DIETRICH

FARCA   791
         .4302
         8
         D251H

HOUSTON PUBLIC LIBRARY
CENTRAL LIBRARY

5/08